A Birmingham Girl Grows Up

Susie Williams

A Birmingham Girl Grows Up

First published as a Kindle e book September 2017

This Paperback Edition November 2017

Also by Susie Williams

From Goats to a Garden

The Flowers in my Bouquet

Our Small Stone Cottage in France

Amber Beads and a Blue Dress

The Twisted Rope (Short Stories)

All are available from Amazon Books and other Booksellers

Website: https://susiewilliams.net

email: susiewilliams842@gmail.com

Susie Williams (author) may also be found on Facebook

Contents

List of Illustrations

ACKNOWLEDGMENTS

Many thanks to family members who contributed photographs and to my husband for preparing this book for publication

.

Chapter One
In the Beginning

I was born during the Second World War. Air raid sirens warned nightly of imminent bombing raids and people had to grab a blanket and some food and rush to the nearest shelter, an Anderson shelter in their own garden or a public shelter. Most people would think it was a ridiculous time to choose to have baby.

My mother, Hetty, was a widow with a teenage daughter. After her husband died of cancer in 1938 she kept up with the insurance payments. Leonard called in the afternoons to collect the money and found a lonely and frightened woman. Maybe their affair started when she invited him in for a cup of tea and poured out her woes. A few tears would have led to an arm round her shoulders to comfort her and then one thing led to another and I was the result.

When she found that she was pregnant he wouldn't leave his wife and marry her so she must have been horrified. As her pregnancy began to show, she and her daughter went to stay with friends in Worcester. And it was there that Leonard paid for her to have the baby in a nursing home in August 1942. The baby's birth was to be a closely guarded secret that was hidden even from close family members.

When I traced and met my half-sister Edna sixty years later, I wondered if she had known that her mother had given birth to an illegitimate baby or had I been a secret from her as well as the rest of the family and the neighbours.

'Did you know about me? I asked her.

'Oh yes,' she said, 'I held you in my arms when you were just a few hours old. I never forgot my baby sister and remembered you especially on your birthday every year.'

It was a disgrace to have a baby out of wedlock; initially I was taken back to the family home in Birmingham but when the neighbours started to get inquisitive it was decided that I would have to be adopted.

Edna said,

'After you were taken away it was if you had never been born. The baby was never, ever discussed.'

But of course, I had been born and after I was taken away from my mother I was sent to a foster mother to await adoption. A medical examination a few weeks later showed me to be underweight, with a tendency to rickets and with dreadful sores in the nappy area.

Fortunately, I was only fostered for three months and at the beginning of December 1942 I went to my new home. After three months a court order confirmed that I was adopted and legally the child of my new parents.

Frank and Marjorie Williams had been married for fifteen years. Although they had wanted a family Marjorie had not become pregnant and they had started to talk about adoption, possibly influenced by the fact that close friends had adopted a baby girl.

A relation, I don't remember who it was, told me many years later that my childless mother-to-be was feeling unfulfilled, that she felt her life was lacking something. She was trying to come to terms with the fact that she wouldn't be able to have a child. Was it true that she had been talking of applying to university? Was it true that Frank didn't like the idea of his wife spreading her wings? I've no idea and by the time this idea was mentioned to me it was too late to ask.

Frank was of the generation that liked their wives at home, for it showed he could afford to keep her and that she didn't need to go out to work to supplement the family income. Would he really have gone to the lengths of stopping her furthering her education and following her own interests? Could he have wanted to prevent her from being better educated than he was? I will never know the truth but the decision had been taken and they were at last going to be parents. The adoption had been approved.

I now remember my adoptive father as a frail old man in his nineties, with a receding hair line and liver spots on his hands and face, but then he was forty-two and in his prime. Photographs show him to have been thin, dark haired and full of energy. For many years he sported a small moustache, inexplicably shaving it off when he was in his sixties.

My adoptive mother was not tall, probably about five-foot-three, slim with blue grey eyes. Her hair was mid-chestnut brown before it went grey. As I grew up people used to say how alike we were and then we would look at each other with slightly raised eyebrows as if sharing a hidden joke. Of course, any similarity was purely coincidental for we were not related at all.

They were overjoyed to finally have a baby and were doting but strict parents. There were quite rigid rules in those days for child rearing such as not picking the infant up when it cried after being put into its cot to sleep or if it woke and cried before the allotted feed time. It was thought this would result in a spoilt child. I heard of one mother who propped her baby up at the end of the sofa and even though it was crying she felt it was wrong to pick it up and cuddle it.

Being adopted meant I had to be bottle fed and apparently Dad became quite adept at using a red-hot needle to get the hole in the teat the right size. Later, solids were introduced and carrots, spinach or prunes were laboriously sieved and reduced to a puree; there were no little jars to pick off supermarket shelves in those days. After all her hard work, my mother was not pleased if the spinach puree was spat out when it was presented on a teaspoon. I gather it sometimes was.

Hardly anyone had washing machines in those days so it's no surprise that early potty training was popular. Furthermore, it was well before the days of disposable nappies. Nappies were made of terry towelling and sometimes a softer muslin nappy was placed next to baby's skin. These muslin squares were also very useful for placing over mother's shoulder to catch any dribbles, or worse, when the infant was put there while its back was gently patted to bring up any wind.

An essential item for the nursery was a nappy bucket with a lid. The worst of the contents of the dirty nappies would be swilled down the loo and then the nappies would be left to soak in the bucket until baby was sleeping outside in its pram the next day. The mother would laboriously hand wash the nappies and probably put them in a boiler placed on top of the gas stove to get them thoroughly clean. Many older houses still had a 'copper' in the corner of the kitchen. This was a large built-in tub, made of copper, into which water would be put and a fire lit underneath to boil water in which to wash nappies and other washing. When they were washed, they had to go through the wringer, or mangle, to squeeze out a lot of water.

They were then ready to have 'a good blow' on the line in the garden. A sign of a good housewife in those days was to have a washing line of nappies briskly blowing in the breeze as early as possible in the morning.

Fresh air was very important and infant was wrapped up and put outside in its pram every morning, more or less whatever the weather. In the afternoons, the baby again went into the pram and was taken for a walk. A favourite walk for me in those very early years was to go to the nearby duck pond to feed the ducks which gathered round the edge of the pond quacking when bread was being thrown to them.

From the pond, a stream led through the cricket

field at the back of the house, then through a park where there were tennis courts and under the main road to another park where there was quite a large pond on which people sailed toy yachts.

This was all on Bournville Village Trust Land where there was a pleasant mixture of different styles of houses and green spaces. All the houses had gardens surrounded by beech hedges and along the roads flowering cherry trees were planted. In the spring the hedges lost the brown leaves they had retained through the winter and soft green leaves unfurled from the spiky buds. Some of the cherry trees had heavy pink blooms; others had white blossom and I remember looking up at bees collecting nectar and seeing the blue sky above. It was a very agreeable place in which to spend my early years.

The war years weren't the easiest time for anyone to start to raise a family. During the rest of the war and in the years that followed, there was food rationing. Welfare Orange Juice was obtained from Mother and Baby Clinics. Milk, meat, eggs, tea, sugar, butter and margarine were among the foodstuffs rationed. Many people grew vegetables in their own gardens and some people also had a few chickens, as did my parents and Auntie Gladys, my mother's domineering elder sister. I can remember now the smell of potato peelings and mash being boiled up in her scullery for the chickens. When we visited them, Uncle Len, her round shouldered husband, with his swept back hair shining from generous applications of Brylcream, fag between pursed lips, took me up the garden, to see the hens in their wire netting enclosure. He had a thriving vegetable garden too.

My earliest memory is being held up in my father's arms when the war ended as we watched the celebratory bonfires and fireworks. My parents had lived through two world wars. No one from our immediate family had been killed in the second war but my mother had lost a brother at Ypres in the first war. Dad was just too young to fight in that war.

His older brother, Percy, was in the Royal Flying Corps as a young man. When I first knew him, he was in middle age but he still had the look of a cheeky small boy about him at times and would talk to me as if I was important to him. Maybe I was for he never had any children of his own. Uncle Percy was one of my favourite uncles. Despite his war time experiences, he appeared to be more relaxed than my father.

He must have been less than twenty years old when he was taking to the skies in those flimsy aircraft. His plane crashed twice, once leaving him dangling in a tree. He had nightmares for many years afterwards, what today we would call post-traumatic stress disorder. The young pilots used to drink a lot, whiskey, brandy, anything alcoholic. I suppose it helped them to forget that tomorrow they might die. I remember Uncle telling me that after a drinking session, most probably the next day, they would load up the planes with the empty bottles and dump them the other side of the lines.

In the second war my father was in a reserve occupation, engineering, so didn't have to fight. He was on the staff of a machine tool factory, H.W. Ward in Selly Oak in Birmingham and took his share of duty as a fire watcher on the factory roof during the bombing raids.

My mother volunteered at a First Aid Post and was ready to receive people injured in the raids. Once she heard that a bomb had fallen in the road in which we lived but had to carry on working until her shift was over, not knowing if her home and family had been hit. All was well for us but further down the road the elderly couple who had gone to the air raid shelter when the siren went off found that when the all clear sounded they had no home left. All that remained was the small brown velvet cushion that the old lady had taken with her to sit on.

In 1945 the bonfires and fireworks brought light at the end of five years of blackout. Gradually the lights came back on and when we went to visit Grandma, Dad's mother, on the other side of town it seemed that on each succeeding visit the colourful neon lights were more prolific.

'It was like this before the war with the bright lights,' my mother said. 'It's good to see them again.'

Grandma lived in Handsworth to the north of Birmingham, an area that has seen many changes since those days. Dad and Uncle Percy had grown up there where they had both been choir boys at Holy Trinity Church, Birchfields. Dad used to tell me the story of how, just before choir practice, they used to 'pinch' apples from the greengrocers on the opposite corner to the church and then race into the vestry. Once there they quickly put their white surplices over their heads and looked very angelic. When the harassed greengrocer rushed in to complain to the choir master he couldn't identify which boys had stolen his apples as they all looked so similar and so very angelic.

The Jamia Masjid Mosque has been built on that corner now and can hold two thousand men. It was formerly called the Saddam Hussein Mosque.

This could not have been envisaged when Grandma had her small upstairs flat in a semi-detached house not far away. There was her bedroom, a small bathroom, a tiny kitchen with a table and a gas ring; washing up was done in the bathroom. The over furnished living room was where we sat, often with Uncle Percy and his wife Auntie Madge, to drink tea out of uncomfortable flower-patterned cups that were fluted round the edges.

I think the weekly visit was very much a duty visit; conversation was stilted but Grandma in her mid-seventies, with her health and strength fading, was no doubt glad to see her sons.

To me she remains a hazy memory, just a little old lady with faded brown hair who wore long sleeved dresses made from a silky material. Later when she was quite frail and came to visit us I jumped out at her from behind a door; that didn't go down very well. She was shocked and told me off. Her childhood and any pranks she got up to were long ago, as were the memories of how her drunken father George Etherington, a tenant farmer, chased her and her siblings round the fields in their nightgowns when he came home from the pub.

I don't think either of her daughters-in-law was very fond of her or close to her. Auntie Madge always called her Mrs Williams. Maybe they resented the relationship the widowed mother had with her two sons. I don't know; I was too young to understand. There was a hint that earlier in their marriages she may have interfered.

Auntie Madge had also grown up in Handsworth. She was a bit of a mystery in some ways. She said her father had been a solicitor but on the 1901 census he was a solicitor's clerk yet the family with four daughters had a maid and a children's nurse. Auntie said her father had one of the earliest cars in Birmingham. He died in 1909 and it seems then her mother went to keep house for a man that Auntie used to call Pa Reynolds. I think he was comfortably off and was probably helpful in some way in getting Uncle Percy into the Royal Flying Corps.

Eventually Grandma went into an old people's home not far from where we lived. It was a gloomy place in tones of brown and deep red with heavy furniture and thick curtains to keep out the light. It was the sort of place that made me, as a child, want to talk in whispers.

Old ladies drifted around eerily in the gloom on

the few occasions I went to visit Grandma. One of them was called Miss Horn. In my ignorance, I concluded that was her name because she had a strange pointed protuberance on her chin. Ladies with horns on their chins and the smell of boiled cabbage and maybe something worse hanging on the air made it a frightening place to be in. I wasn't at all keen to be there.

Grandma died when I was about ten. As a child she had lived at Rushbrook Farm near Tanworth-in-Arden. I wish I had known her better as stories from her childhood on the farm in the 1870s and 1880s would have been fascinating but small children are not often interested in their grandparent's history unless the person concerned has a gift for storytelling.

Those journeys across town in the 1940s to Handsworth revealed many bomb sites, gaping holes and piles of broken bricks between rows of terraced houses and small shops. To me it seemed almost as if we had gone to another planet. This was an alien world, far removed from the leafy suburb in which I was growing up.

As the years went on, mauve buddleia bushes surrounded by clouds of butterflies colonised the bomb sites and flourished among the dereliction. Mother Nature was bringing beauty to where there had been death and violence.

The end of rationing was still many years away and my parents continued to keep hens in the garden to provide us with eggs. Seeing the brown hens looking at me when I was sitting in my pram is another early memory.

My parents had acquired a Springer Spaniel brought back from Cornwall before the war. They called her Polo, apparently after seeing a game of water polo from the cliffs above Mevagissey on a camping holiday. During my childhood, Polo had several litters of puppies, gorgeous soft wriggly little creatures, crawling over and under each other in their eagerness to be picked up and cuddled.

Auntie Fowler and Uncle Charlie, a childless couple, lived next door. They were not related to me in any way but in those days the friends of one's parents were always called Auntie or Uncle, courtesy aunts and uncles we said. Uncle Charlie had been blown up in the First World War but had survived, though profoundly deaf ever since. I don't think he could hear what I said when I was chattering away in toddler-speak but he had a lovely smile, albeit with the odd tooth missing, and twinkly eyes, so that was alright.

His wife's name was Elizabeth but goodness knows why I called her Auntie Fowler, which was her surname; maybe she thought that calling her Auntie Elizabeth would be too familiar. She was a very gracious lady and the sofa in her south facing sitting room was covered in a beautiful flowery chintz fabric. To stop it fading she kept the curtains closed most of the time. I have a faint memory of the smell of that room. I wonder if it was pot pourri or moth balls? Whatever it was, the room was fresh and a delight to be in. I can see her now holding a bone china tea cup, little finger extended elegantly, as she and my mother chatted over a cup of Lapsang Suchong.

Auntie Flo and Uncle Walter also featured in my early years. Again, they were not related to my parents. Uncle Walter was the registrar at Lodge Hill Cemetery, Selly Oak, Birmingham between 1927 and 1951 and they lived in the house at the entrance to the cemetery. My mother often walked me the half mile up the hill to visit them. In their living room the fireplace surround was made of painted tiles and on the wall was a print of a painting by a Dutch artist. On warm days we would relax in the garden where I sat on a folding wooden stool that once collapsed and pinched my fingers.

I have very loving memories of that gentle Quaker couple. Uncle Walter was in the Labour Corps during the First World War which was composed of men who had been injured in battle and were medically unfit to return to the front line. But it was also the place were conscientious objectors served. I suspect Uncle Walter, as a Quaker, was in the latter category. This was in no way a soft option as they were often labouring right in the line of battle.

Later Uncle Walter had a stroke and couldn't speak clearly. I thought it was a great game to play school with him when I was a small child and try to get him to talk properly. No one stopped me doing that. Maybe it was thought helpful to him in the recovery of his speech. Auntie Flo was a dear lady, who suffered without complaint her handicap of being a hunch back.

Their Christianity was of the quiet practical kind. Before meals no verbal grace was said but heads were bowed silently for a few moments as each person gave thanks to God. There was no ostentation in their home but there was a lot of love.

Before his stroke Uncle drove a modest car, probably an Austin Seven, and I remember once as a small child I sat in the passenger seat when the door flew open as we went along. There were no child seats or safety belts in those days and he just calmly leant across me and pulled the door to as he continued to drive.

I was a very curious child, always asking questions.

'Where do babies come from Mummy?'

'They come from their mummies' tummies,' she replied.

She had a feeling that the question she'd known she would have to answer one day was coming soon and it did. A few days later, when I had digested that interesting fact, I went back with another question.

'So, I came from your tummy, did I?'

'Well, no you didn't. You were specially chosen instead.'

And thus, I learnt that I was adopted but that never worried me. I was specially chosen and that gave me quite a boost. I was important.

I didn't need to know anything else at that stage but as the years unfolded the questions about my origins were answered openly. I was told then that my natural mother was a widow and I was born as a result of her affair with a married man and that having an illegitimate baby was a disgrace so after a short while I was sent away to be adopted.

I was also told that my natural mother already had a daughter. This fact was stored away and simmered in the back of my mind for the next sixty years. When I was forty-seven I obtained my original birth certificate and later, after my adoptive parents had died, I started tracing my natural mother. When I obtained her death certificate I found my sister's name. She had been present at the death; there also was her address and I discovered by looking at the electoral roll that she was still alive.

Being adopted wasn't particularly unusual in my world. My godparents had three adopted children; other close friends of my parents had adopted a boy whom they called Peter. Initially my mother had wanted to adopt a boy as well, a brother for me, but coping with just one child apparently was enough. So, an only child I remained.

A few years later I saw a long line of children walking in twos and wearing identical uniforms. My mother told me they were from a nearby orphanage. These were among the many illegitimate war-time babies and orphans who had not been adopted, who had not been as fortunate as I had been in having a loving home. My heart went out to them and it was then that I resolved to adopt a child or children myself when I was grown up.

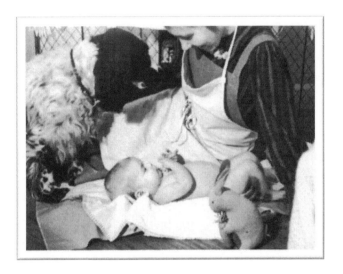

1. Susie aged three months

2. Christening Day, April 1943

3. Susie with her parents and Polo the dog.

4. Grandma

*5. Susie with Cousin Eric just before
the end of the war*

6. Susie enjoyed rides on her father's bicycle

7. Polo's puppies

Chapter Two
A Change of Scene

When I was about five we moved to live in a detached house in South Road, Northfield. The roads without trees, the gardens with fences but no hedges and the lack of nearby parks made the area less attractive than the surroundings of the previous house. I can only think that the lure of a detached rather than a semi-detached house prompted the move. I was now five and so there are a lot more memories of the next few years.

We moved to Northfield in the spring of 1947 and I started school in the Autumn. A small private school called 'Rathvilly' on Bunbury Road had been chosen for me. I remember it as being rather a bleak place but that may have been due to that winter being extraordinarily cold and the shortage of coal for heating. I suspect I didn't much like the toilets there either because on the way home my mother frequently had to take me behind a gravestone in St Laurence's churchyard to attend to a call of nature and afterwards down the steep stone steps and past the old dog pound.

To combat the cold, I wore a liberty bodice over my woollen vest. Liberty bodices, those strange shapeless garments with lines of webbing and rubber suspenders to hold up woollen stockings, were invented at the end of the nineteenth century as an alternative to the corset. Sometimes known then as the emancipation bodice. Yes, now I understand, 'emancipation', liberty from the dreaded corset.

One day at school I stuck my tongue out at another child. The teacher caught me at my dastardly deed and my punishment was to go behind the free-standing blackboard with my tongue stuck out for twenty minutes. A good example I think of the punishment being made to fit the crime. I probably decided not to stick my tongue out again. I do remember it ached for a while afterwards.

At the side of the school was a pleasant field bounded by a line of large beech trees. Sports Day was held there in the summer term. This small girl was in the race doing forward rolls and resolutely gambolled diagonally across the field thus ending up nowhere near the finishing line but at her mother's feet. How embarrassing.

Although we did a lot of gluing I have no memories of the works of art that we were attempting to create but I do remember the almondy smell of the glue. Funny isn't it how certain smells bring back memories. And I remember the cold wash room and the line of basins where hands were washed in cold water and dried on nearly wet towels.

In the summer term, I was allowed to walk home with a slightly older girl who lived in the same road as we did. Petrol was still rationed and there were far fewer cars around so the roads were much safer than they are today. Children walked to and from school, often on their own. They never got ferried there in cars although sometimes when they were very young their mothers walked to school with them. My husband, as a five-year-old, went by himself to the centre of Nottingham on one bus, changed to another and went to his school on that. No wonder he grew up to be so independent.

No doubt my mother had told me that I must always go straight home but in the summer term, on one memorable day when I walked home with a friend, I went home with her to look at her goldfish. When I finally arrived home one look at my mother's face told me I was in trouble.

'Where have you been?' she asked me.

'Glenys said I could go and look at her goldfish.'

'Did I say you could go and look at Glenys's goldfish?'

No reply.

'Look at me. Did I say you could go and look at the goldfish or did I tell you to always come straight home?'

'You told me to come straight home.'

'Have you been a naughty, disobedient girl?'

'I've been a naughty, disobedient girl.'

'I'm sending you to your room to think about how naughty you have been. Go on. Upstairs with you and stay there until I call you down.'

Being sent to my room was my usual punishment; a bit like being put on the 'naughty step' as today's children are. In my bedroom there were delights in the form of books and I very much doubt that I spent much time reflecting on my wickedness.

I was an avid reader even at that age so it wasn't such a hard punishment as it might have been. The white painted bookshelf that my father had made for me was next to my bed and I still have that book shelf today. It held my favourite books - Winnie the Pooh, Now We Are Six, When We Were Very Young, Alice in Wonderland, all the Little Grey Rabbit books and many others. Some of them are still on it to this day and my own children read these books too.

It was only two years after the war when we went to live in the house at Northfield and all the way down the roadside were metal pig bins into which people were encouraged to put left over food and vegetable peelings. Nothing was wasted and I doubt if much food was actually left over. I was never allowed to leave any food on my plate. If I didn't eat it I had to sit there staring at it congealing and becoming cold. Sometimes I sat there for a considerable time. I don't remember it coming out again for the next meal or even for breakfast the following day, but I know these are the memories some people have.

Another waste product that my father was keen not to miss out on was the horse manure deposited in the road by the milkman's horse. The milk was still being delivered by horse and cart. He and a neighbour would often meet out there, armed with their galvanised buckets and a shovel to scoop up the horse's offerings which made a valuable addition to the vegetable garden. Dad grew a lot of fruit and vegetables, very necessary if you wanted to eat a good diet as there were still serious shortages in those post war years.

Dad had some cousins who lived in British Columbia and each Christmas, while rationing lasted, they sent us a food parcel. There were tins of butter and peaches but most welcome of all to me was the box of Peak Freans iced biscuits. There was very little sugar in my life. My mother was very keen that I should grow up eating a healthy diet and I didn't taste chocolate until my first day at school when I was given a piece as a treat.

Christmases just after the war were very simple occasions. Gifts for relations were homemade. My mother and I sat in the front room before the fire glimmering behind the glazed doors of a type of room heater and I cut out pictures from magazines and stuck them onto card with a tiny calendar. A piece of wall paper on the back and a ribbon loop for the top completed the job and behold, there was a present for an aunt or uncle.

We also went out into the countryside and collected empty beech nut cases which were painted with enamel paint, put in groups of two or three and somehow turned into a brooch. All my aunts and uncles were the recipients of these small homemade gifts into which a lot of concentration and effort had gone. There was no recourse to shop-bought presents. It was the thought that counted and, of course, the effort.

Decorations were homemade too with coloured paper being cut into strips which were then glued together and inter linked to make attractive paper chains. Holly and mistletoe for draping over pictures came in from the countryside and thus the house was ready for Christmas.

As a small child, I remember being taken to visit Father Christmas in his grotto at Lewis's, a big department store in town. It was a very popular thing to do just before Christmas. When I was seven I went to Dudley Zoo with my cousin Mary and was photographed riding on Santa's sleigh, behind a large stuffed reindeer.

I always found a stocking from Father Christmas at the end of my bed on Christmas morning. There was a coconut sticking out of the top, an orange in the toe and in between numerous tiny presents like pencils, rubbers and crayons. It was all so simple but just as much fun, if not more so than the extravagant presents of today.

One year I had a magnificent present. It was a large grey wooden box containing small models of farm animals and hay carts. My father had made the box and various farm buildings such as a cart shed and a pig sty, which were in the box and he had painted the underside of the lid with green fields and a track running through them. I loved playing with my farm and then, many years later, doing it for real on our smallholding although a neighbouring farmer friend warned me then that,

'You're only playing at farming you know!' He was quite right as our few animals then were not our main source of income.

Not only did that box contain my toy farm; there were various percussion instruments as well; a drum, a tambourine, some castanets and a xylophone. What fun I had with all of these things. As an only child, I had to amuse myself lot of the time.

One Christmas I was given a doll called Rosebud by my parents. Rosebud had none of the attributes of today's dolls. She wasn't soft, she didn't cry 'Mama' and she didn't wee. But I loved her even though she was hard and her arms and legs were stiff. She came with a blue knitted dress, coat, knickers and bootees that my mother had made for her. There was another present too. From Auntie Madge there was a whole wardrobe of clothes that she had made. There was a silky lace-edged nightdress, and other knitted and fabric dresses and coats. There was a pretty blue flowery dress made from a Viyella fabric with knickers to match and knitted vests as well and bootees. I spent ages dressing and undressing Rosebud while she carried on a conversation with Teddy, a straw-filled bear made by my mother. I can almost imagine myself, looking back all those years, chattering away to myself and my dolls with my blond curls bobbing up and down and my child like voice going on and on.

A Christmas present I didn't particularly like was a pair of gloves made by someone my mother knew who kept dogs. The dogs had been combed and their hair incorporated into knitting wool and made into gloves. They were light brown and they itched; very different from a jumper I once knitted many years later from wool I had spun from a Jacob fleece given to me by my cousin Mary. It was so soft all my friends wanted to stroke it when my husband wore it.

For some unknown reason a couple called Mr and Mrs Paget lived with us for a while using the spare front bedroom. To me they became 'Uncle' Ernest and 'Auntie' Katy.

Uncle Ernest, neatly suited and with a rolled umbrella, went off on the bus each day to work at an office in Birmingham which left Auntie Katy with not a lot to do except wash her hair set it in parallel lines of waves and paint her nails.

She wanted to give me a treat one day so she took me to the Lickey Hills on the tram. Sitting on a bench in the woods, she plied me with chocolate biscuits, afterwards carefully wiping the melted chocolate from my hands with a handkerchief.

Of course, I thought this unaccustomed food was delicious but my mother had a very different view of the episode when she found out about it. She was furious. That sort of food was not on the list of acceptable food for me. I don't think the Pagets lasted long after that episode.

While we lived there our dog Polo had puppies again and I have a photo of me aged about six holding a wriggling puppy.

I acquired a dear little tabby kitten who led a charmed life until being accidently run over by a neighbour, after we had moved to another house, when her car reversed over the sleeping cat.

We also had three ducks which we eventually ate. I spent a lot of time digging up worms in the garden and chopping them into bits for the ducks to eat. How gruesome! The ducks were all in favour of the idea.

My father, who had spent part of his childhood on his grandfather's farm near Tanworth-in-Arden killed the ducks when they were large enough to eat. The largest duck was called Donald. How original! Donald was larger than the other two ducks and my father used to recall the soulful look in Donald's eyes when he finally went to wring his neck.

While we lived at that house, my parents became friendly with Arthur and Joan who lived on the opposite side of the road. They had a son called Jeremy who was two years younger than I was. The friendship was not improved by me hitting him over the head with a box one day. I suppose I was not getting my own way over some game we were playing. Poor Jeremy. His father took my hand and marched me home. His mother went to bed with a headache. How embarrassing, I think now, but was I then? Probably not, just cross at not getting my own way and having to suffer the indignity of being marched down the road and having to listen to my father being regaled with my sins.

Funnily enough I don't remember that they

became Uncle Arthur and Auntie Joan. Maybe you didn't encourage a child who had battered your one and only adored son to be that familiar.

Every Christmas a scene from one of the Little Grey Rabbit stories was erected in the bay window of their sitting room. With cut-out figures of the Hare, the Squirrel and the Little Grey Rabbit, these tableaux were delightful despite the slight smell of mildew they had acquired through being stored in the loft.

Eventually the family moved to live in Cardiff and later we went to visit them. The box incident had obviously been put on the back burner. On Sunday morning, the joint of meat for lunch was put in the oven and off we all went in the car to see the local beauty spots. Joan kept looking at her watch and became increasing concerned about the meat becoming overcooked. Sure enough, when the front door was opened on our return the smell of burnt food and blue smoke wafted out. Some smells stay with you for ever and that is one of them.

The other day I found a telegram from Jeremy, sent on my wedding day.

'Sorry I can't be with you,' it said. I don't know where he was but his parents came to my wedding and Joan, elegant as always, wore a fur stole.

I became friendly with Diana who lived next door and Hilary who lived opposite to us. I must have been about eight at the time and they were a year or so older. We decided to raise some money for the RSPCA. We made items to sell, local people baked cakes and biscuits and these items were placed on a table in front of the garage door. Neighbours rallied round to swell the funds we were sending to that animal charity. We even had our picture in The Birmingham Mail.

Soon after that Hilary moved away with her family; a Scottish family, the Murdochs, came to live there. They had two daughters, Patricia and Margaret, and eventually, after I had left Rathvilly, we went to school together on the tram. I clearly remember an incident when Dad took all three of us to school in his car. I was still biting my nails at that time and he grabbed one of my hands and held it up in front of Patricia and Margaret. He'd noticed that they didn't bite their nails,

'Look, you could have nice nails too if you didn't bite them,' he said scathingly, but that didn't help one bit. Sometime later I suddenly realised I had actually given up biting my nails. That wasn't the only occasion Dad was to compare me to someone else, to my detriment. Not good at confidence building was my father!

In those days Gypsy women came around the streets from time to time selling pegs and little bundles of lavender. My mother used to make cups of tea for them and these women came into the covered yard at the side of the house to sit and drink them.

'Good Luck to you lady,' they'd say through a mouthful of ill-assorted teeth as they left. 'Here's some lucky heather for you'.

I even remember an Onion Johnny coming down

the road with strings of onions hanging from the handle bars of his bike. How exotic, all the way from Brittany.

It was from the covered yard that my father emerged into the kitchen on one of my birthdays. My birthday present was crawling up his tie. It was a white mouse. What on earth prompted that gift I wonder? Maybe I had seen one in a pet shop window and oohed and aahed over it. When I fast forward to later years and recollect my efforts to exterminate rats and mice I find it quite amazing to think I had one as a pet. I remember nothing of its impact on me or the household except perhaps the acrid smell emanating from its cage when it needed cleaning out. Who cleaned it out? I don't know but maybe it was bought for me to teach me how to be responsible for the welfare of a small animal. In later years I had plenty of large animals to clean out, including goats and pigs, but I can't by any stretch of the imagination think that owning a white mouse when I was eight prepared me for that.

The kitchen in that detached house was in many ways the centre of the home. I think they often are. A fire in a black-leaded grate, burned there in the winter. It was a coal fire and to keep it in, either when we went out or overnight, it had to be 'backed-up' with slack. Slack being very small pieces of coal, more like gravel really, put in a bucket and mixed with water. The slow-burning fire was carefully covered with this mixture patted onto it with a shovel, rather in the style of charcoal burners plugging all the gaps with smaller and smaller pieces of wood.

I used to sit by the fire listening to children's hour on the wireless when I came home from school. Uncle Mac talked over the air-waves to us. I loved the series called 'Said the Cat to the Dog' about Momty and Peckam, which had a very catchy signature tune. And there was Toy Town with Larry the Lamb and Mr Mayor and the Just So Stories too. The thing about radio was that you could let your imagination have full rein. It was wonderful. I had a very good imagination.

In one corner of the kitchen was a sink and draining board with a gas cooker close by. On the other side of the room was a dresser with glass doors and below them a pull-down flap on which pastry could be made; there were cupboards underneath it.

There was also a walk-in pantry surrounded by shelves where jam and bottled fruit were stored. Jam making and fruit bottling in those pre-freezer days were an essential task for the post-war housewife. On the floor was a bulky pancheon containing eggs preserved in isinglass and a large tin containing boiled sweets which, by the time you got to the bottom, had all congealed into a solid sticky mass. These were produced on visiting days and taken to my mother's Aunt Lizzie who was in Selly Oak Hospital. Occasionally I was allowed to have one.

In the centre of the kitchen was a square table and this was where we had our meals. In those pre-central heating days, the kitchen was the one room in the house which was usually warm. There was a blue painted rocking chair by the fire with flowery cushions that matched the curtains.

I was a rather cheeky child and once, when I went too far in my father's opinion, he tried to give me a slap. He chased me round and round the kitchen table getting more and more irate and still trying to whack me. Unfortunately for him he ended up whacking the table and I escaped my punishment that day. In later years, we laughed about the incident. He reckoned he'd broken his finger.

I don't think I was often smacked but I did tell lies and was punished in some way for that. However, by the time I was nine I decided it was better to face up to telling the truth. I concluded that the punishment for lying was far worse than the punishment for whatever my misdeeds were, usually being cheeky and answering back I expect. Yes, I did a lot of that, sometimes losing my 3d a week pocket money for weeks on end.

My bedroom was at the back of the house and at night I could hear the trains being shunted in the goods yard about half a mile away. Further away but still audible were the presses at the Austin factory at Longbridge going bang, bang in the night. Often my bedroom window was open and one night there was a terrific gale and it blew off and crashed down onto the terrace below. Boards were hammered over the gap and when I woke up in the morning I wondered what had happened. I had slept through the whole episode.

Much more pleasant were the evenings when I

had been put to bed and was able to listen to my father playing the piano in the sitting room. He was a very accomplished pianist and had been given piano lessons as a child. Before the First World War he used to play the piano for the children at his school when they marched into assembly. Later he sometime played for the silent films at the local cinema. He was born in 1900 so was just a Victorian. I used to think that accounted for a lot.

In my childhood he enjoyed having musical evenings with his friends and a trio was formed. Dad played the piano, a dear old man called Mr Hooson, with a droopy moustache and horn-rimmed glasses, played his cello. He came from Halifax and had a Yorkshire accent. Another man played the violin. I loved listening to them as I gradually drifted off to sleep.

On other occasions Dad played his Bechstein upright grand piano on his own and whenever I hear Beethoven's Moonlight Sonata I am transported back to those evenings when I lay in bed listening to that wonderful music. I think it gave him a sense of power to play the music as loudly as he could, not I think what Beethoven intended especially regarding the Moonlight Sonata.

When I was nine my mother took me to a concert at Birmingham Town Hall to hear the pianist Moiseiwitsch play. He was born in the Ukraine in 1890. I found the experience of the concert entrancing for there was this amazing man playing incredible music from memory. Later, in my teenage years, I went to many classical music concerts in the Town Hall.

Music was not the only love in my life. I soon developed a love of the countryside which has stayed with me all my life. During the war my parents had discovered a farm at Hanbury near Droitwich which took in paying guests and it was where they stayed for a few days every now and then to have a break from the bombing in Birmingham. This continued after the war and sometimes my mother would take me there for a week with Dad joining us at the weekends.

The farm was owned by Jack and Dorothy Heard who lived there with two grown-up daughters, Joan and Sheila. By the fire in the kitchen was an easy chair where Jack Heard sat in the evenings after a hard day out on the farm. I remember seeing him there after he'd had fallen from his race-horse, Noffy, after a point to point race at Worcester. I remember him as a rather silent man, but then you would be after an accident; at other times he was known to crack a joke and give a wry laugh. Dorothy Heard was always busy and wearing a pinafore. Busy cooking meals for visitors, busy feeding her chickens and washing the eggs, busy preparing bread and milk for the semi-wild cats that lived in the barn and a million other tasks that being a farmer's wife entailed.

When I was quite a small child Joan Heard was married and the wedding was held in the beautiful old church on the hill at Hanbury where each of the pews had its own door. The church was later to become famous as the church where Grace and Phil Archer married. When Joan came into the church for her wedding I was so keen to see the bride walk down the aisle with her father that I leaned on the pew door which burst open and deposited me at the bride's feet. I gather it was regarded as an amusing incident although I expect my mother was highly embarrassed.

The red-brick farmhouse was very old fashioned; when I first went there electricity had not been installed so I think there must just have been oil lamps. Cooking was done on oil stoves in the kitchen. I remember that there were two of them with burners on the top and ovens below. They produced a not totally unpleasant smoky smell.

I don't think I was allowed in the kitchen when meals were being cooked but I remember the enamel bowls of cream sitting on the top of the stoves over a low, gentle heat being turned into golden clotted cream. Even writing about it now is making my mouth water.

From the back door near the duck pond one entered a large back hall off which were the kitchen, the farm office and the room where the eggs were set out and the milk was left to stand so that the cream rose to the top. I suppose it was called the dairy. In the kitchen was an open fire, a large table and chairs where the family ate; also a sink and the oil stoves.

Visitors ate in the dining room which was at the front of the house. Across the hall, from where stairs led to the bedrooms, there was a sitting room.

Italian prisoners of war were working on the land in those early years straight after the war. When they saw families staying at the farm they must have thought nostalgically of their families at home. They were repatriated quite soon after that and no doubt were thankful to get back to their homeland and their own families.

It was a traditional mixed farm where some horses were still used although tractors had just started to make an appearance. There were powerful cart horses, riding horses and ponies. There were cows, pigs, sheep and poultry. Field beans and wheat were grown and there was grazing land. That type of mixed farm is rarely seen today.

There were wild flower meadows where the grass was harvested for hay. I used to walk there with my mother, the Observers Book of Wild Flowers in hand, while she taught me the names of the flowers. What fascinating names they have, the Scarlet Pimpernel that opens when the sun shines, Ragged Robin and Cranesbill among many others.

When the hay was ready it was cut and turned several times then put in stooks until it was dry, a process totally dependent on the weather. Damp hay would go mouldy and be useless. Thus, wet summers were disastrous for the farmers leaving them with no hay for the winter feed. All being well, eventually it was stored in the hay loft above the stables where it scented the air with the smell of summer pastures. When needed it was pushed down into the hay racks below for the horses.

At the front of the farmhouse there was a low wall between the house and the large farm-yard. The wall was home to many snails that lived under the yellow corydalis that grew there.

On the left-hand side of the yard were the wooden stables where the horses and ponies were kept. It occurs to me that this was a huge fire risk and reminds me of the scene in Black Beauty where the hotel stables caught fire and where, after he had been rescued, Black Beauty heard the dying screams of the two horses that could not be saved in time. The fire had been caused by a man smoking a pipe in the hay loft.

On the other side of the yard was a large barn and the tack room. The barn housed farm machinery and was where the steam driven threshing machine came once a year at harvest time. It was a busy time. A reaper-binder had cut the ripe, golden wheat and tied it into sheaves which were then, like the hay, put into stooks to dry. Later the sheaves of wheat were tossed high onto a cart with a pitchfork and taken to the barn to await the arrival of the noisy threshing machine and steam engine.

As a small girl, I had to be kept well out of the way of dangerous machinery, pitchforks and busy farm workers but I remember it being a fascinating sight. The sheaves were put on a conveyer belt which took the wheat into the machine which separated the grain from the wheat stalks. The wheat stalks became the straw which was a valuable commodity for animal bedding. The wheat grain was sent away to be milled into flour and the straw was stacked in the barn or in a straw stack outside.

The barn was also home to countless cats. They were fed on bread and milk which was brought out to the farm-yard in old meat tins. As soon as the food appeared cats would come from every direction for their bread and milk. They were essential on the farm to keep the rat and mouse population down.

The tack room was a joy to behold. It held the saddles and bridles, bits, brushes and curry combs, horse blankets and horse brasses and all the other paraphernalia associated with riding. Along the wall was a line of rosettes denoting the number of races and events that had been won in competitive events. There was also a very evocative smell of saddle soap and polish. A wonderful place.

How different life on the farm was then, nearly seventy-five years ago. Today combine harvesters do all the tasks of the reaper binder, and threshing machine and are guided by GPS cutting out much of the manual labour associated with the harvesting of those days. Cleaning out stables and cow sheds is done by machine, milking by hand is in the distant past, electricity is everywhere and the internet has revolutionised life in the country as well as the town. I don't suppose there is any less pressure on our farmers though as they deal with quotas, watch closely as prices fluctuate and endure endless bureaucracy.

It's probably a lonelier life today than it was then,

as farmers spend hours alone in a tractor cab and farm office. Some studies have found that farmers are three times more likely to take their own lives than people in other professions. All those years ago more labour would have been employed and there would have been more human interaction. To me as a small child, life on the farm and in the countryside, was wonderful.

The Heards were a very horsey family and apart from the working horses still used on the farm after the war there were riding horses and ponies which took part in point-to-point races, gymkhanas and fox-hunting. Two of the ponies I remember being allowed to ride were Snowy and Lassie. Jack Heard used his horse 'Off Chance' to race in the Point to Point Races at Worcester and I remember Sheila, their younger daughter, going off riding around the lanes and sometimes taking a tumble and coming back with a grazed chin.

As members of the local hunt they 'walked' two fox hound puppies every year which meant that the puppies lived with them for the first year of their lives; then they went off to join the other hounds in the hunt kennels. They were delightful dogs, always getting into trouble as puppies do and, of course, they lived outside, not in the farmhouse. They were not pets but, as the photo of two of them with my mother shows, they were not averse to a bit of petting.

If we were staying there when there was a Hunt we used to follow it, as did a wide range of people. We went on foot while the hunt members rode beautiful hunters and wore their hunting pink jackets; others followed riding an assortment of ponies and horses; some followed on bicycles too.

Until electricity came to that part of rural Worcestershire the cows were milked by hand. There was a dairy around the corner from the stables and I watched with great interest as the milk, warm from the cows, was poured into the top of a cooler that had a cold-water core down the middle. Then it went into churns, some to be collected and taken into Worcester, and some to be used in the house. Some of the wonderful creamy milk was set aside in wide enamel bowls for the cream to rise and then put on a very low heat on top of the oil stoves to be turned into clotted cream. When we went to stay at the farm there were delicious puddings with cooked fruit, pies and lots of clotted cream. The fruit came from the farm's orchards where apples, plums and pears were grown. Blackberries were picked from the hedgerows. Some of the hens sometimes 'laid away' meaning they went off to a hidden spot in a hedgerow and a whole clutch of eggs would turn up where least expected.

Breakfasts were porridge, home-reared bacon and farm-fresh free-range eggs. The milk was whole and unpasteurised. This was very different from the usual post war diet during rationing, thanks to the availability of all this wonderful food on the farm.

I don't remember wet days. The sun always shines in childhood or so it seems looking back to that time seventy years ago. The days at the farm were full of sunshine and beautiful surroundings. I awoke in the morning to the peaceful sound of pigeons cooing, unaware at that time of my life that they are generally regarded as a pest as they eat the farmer's crops. Once I remember I had to sleep in Sheila's bedroom; maybe the house was full of guests. Covertly I watched her, through half-closed eyes, getting dressed in the morning and pulling a shirt over her blossoming curves.

Sometimes I could ride one of the ponies, as did the Caddy girls who also stayed at the farm with their parents. They always had loads of sweets with them as Grandfather Caddy owned a sweet making factory.

I rode Snowy, a little white Shetland pony but my mother was always alongside making sure Snowy didn't run away with me. Snowy did choose to run one day when we were walking over a 'ridge and furrow' field. There was my poor mother hanging on for grim life as we bounced up and then down the wide furrows. That bit of the farm must have been a remnant of the three-field system of medieval times when each serf had an allocated number of strips to farm. It was near a stream so that would have been a good water supply for their crops.

The tree-lined stream meandered across another field as did we on our walks. At bedtime, my mother was reading Wind in the Willows to me and so I was on the lookout for magical scenes. I found secret fairy steps where tree roots made a short staircase down to the water's edge in the dappled shade. There must have been fairies and water sprites there I was sure.

We walked in the hay meadows on the other side of the farm with our wild flower book and butterfly book in hand. Nature's classroom was very enjoyable. Butterflies and bees were prolific and as we wandered by the hedgerows the wheel of the metal windmill near the farmhouse blew round above us pumping water from deep underground for the farm.

The arrival of my father at the weekend boded the end of the holiday but before that the Heards and their house visitors played tennis on the grass court near the drive.

I went back a few years ago. The tennis court was long gone and the line of stables, where I had smelt sweet hay, was collapsing. More recently I see on Google Earth that all the old farm buildings have gone now and have been replaced by ugly aluminium sheds and barns. How sad.

That farm near Droitwich was half way between Birmingham and Worcester where my parents lived before the war. At first, a long time before they adopted me, they lived in rented accommodation in the St John's area of Worcester but in about 1930 moved to an isolated rural cottage near the hamlet of Warndon. I remember from later visits, when I was a small child, a rutted lane, a farm yard, hens pecking the earth for grubs and a pretty white church with box pews. That was before a huge housing estate was built there. Today Warndon is the name of a motorway service station on the M5.

At the cottage there was no indoor plumbing and the toilet was an earth closet at the end of the garden. My parents had worked out that if they lived there the rent would be lower and they would be able to save up to have the house of their dreams built in Tolladine Road.

This they did in 1936 and became friendly with Deanie and Bill Allen who lived just up the road. Auntie Deanie was a small lady with a squint and a slightly lop-sided appearance. I think she had come from a rather 'good' family who lived somewhere in eastern England, on the Fens possibly, and in the home in Worcester were pieces of oak furniture and pictures from her childhood home. I have a large blue Willow pattern type meat platter on the wall at our French cottage that came from her and is a pleasant reminder of the visits to her home with my mother. From her bathroom window was a view of Bredon Hill not far away and once while I was in their garden a Lancaster Bomber flew over, its heavy throbbing engines such an evocative sound.

Uncle Bill was a taciturn man who spent hours tending his vegetable garden. Neatly mown grass paths ran between tidy, well-hoed rows of vegetables and nearer to the house was a smooth lawn.

Like my parents at the time they had no children, neither did they ever have any. During the school holidays when my father went to Worcester on business each week my mother and I often went to visit Auntie Deanie while Uncle Bill, like my father, was at work.

She once told my mother that while the two of them were chatting I kept kicking her gently. It seems I was jealous and felt I wasn't getting enough attention. What an obnoxious child I was.

Poor Auntie Deanie, her life with Uncle Bill can't have been easy. Many years later she died of the effects on her liver of alcoholism. My mother was astonished and found this difficult to believe as she had never seen any bottles lying around.

At the bottom of the hill near her home was a dairy selling milk and nearby was the bus stop from which it was a short ride into Worcester.

I was rather pleased, in later years when I was researching my natural family, to discover that I had been born in Worcester.

We used to go into the town sometimes and I particularly remember visits to the Cathedral. After walking along the High Street, the road passed a row of tall Georgian houses. One of them often had its front door open and on the shiny parquet hall floor there was a spinning wheel. It looked so inviting.

A few more steps led to the cathedral entrance, dark after the brightness outside. After pushing through the heavy door, it was so quiet, in contrast to the noise of the busy streets. One's senses became more alert because it wasn't just the calm atmosphere and the huge space that one was suddenly aware of but the smell of wax polish and the light filtering down from the beautiful Rose Window at the western end of the building.

I grew to love that place and almost always when I visited Worcester as a child and in later years, made sure I visited the Cathedral, perched high above the River Severn.

It was founded in 680 and during Anglo-Saxon times was known as one of the most important monastic cathedrals in the country. Apparently the undercroft of the old monastery today houses an important colony of bats.

My mother nurtured my interest in its history as we wandered round and explored; the Cloisters where the monks had walked and worked; the Chapter House, the ornately carved 15th century misericords in the choir where the monks had stood for the midnight services and the tomb of bad King John situated in front of the High Altar. I wondered how a bad king could end up in such a wonderful place. In 1540 Henry the Eighth dissolved the monastery and in the Civil War the cathedral was badly damaged.

I often regret that my mother and I in my teenage years did not have a very good relationship but in writing about these early memories I realise thankfully how much she gave me in terms of my love of nature, music and history.

When I was older we went to a performance of Elgar's Dream of Gerontius in Worcester Cathedral during the Three Choirs Festival. Each year a choir composed of singers from Hereford, Gloucester and Worcester took it in turn to perform in one of the three cathedrals. We had seats in the choir stalls and faced down the nave to where a stage had been erected for the choir to sing beneath the beautiful Rose window. It was just amazing to sit there listening to that wonderful music reverberating around the ancient pillars and arches and rising to the vaulted ceiling. This brought back memories for my parents who had sung in the Three Choirs Festival when they lived in Worcester before the war.

On my childhood visits into Worcester and to the Cathedral, Auntie Deanie often accompanied us. Sometimes we sat in the sun in a sheltered corner of the grounds but when Auntie discovered it was popular with large furry caterpillars we moved on. I loved to watch them though.

We used to walk through the terraced gardens and peer over the stone wall to see the swans floating on the river below. Sometimes they would be near to the red sandstone bridge dating from 1781. I was interested to read recently that the bridge it replaced was constructed with a central tower, like the one that still exists at Monmouth.

Steps led down from the gardens to the Water Gate which gave access onto the path that ran alongside the river. By the side of the Water Gate numerous plaques denote the river levels during the many times the river has overflowed its banks. The County Cricket ground opposite the Water Gate usually floods at such times. Returning up the Water Gate steps you get to College Green and thence to the

Edgar Tower the only remaining part of Worcester Castle. Passing through that the road leads out of the Cathedral Precincts and back towards the town. I was fascinated by the holes in the underside of the roof of the Edgar Tower. My mother told me that during the Civil War boiling lead was poured through those holes onto the heads of the enemy. Ouch! Apparently the first and the last battles of the Civil War were fought near Worcester.

My own war wounds occurred in Auntie Deanie's garden when I was about six.

One day I fell over Auntie's black spaniel while I was running down one of the grass paths and unfortunately landed up on some barbed wire and gashed the inner side of my knee rather badly. I had to be taken to see a doctor in Worcester. The knee was bandaged up and we caught the bus into town.

It was about two o'clock in the afternoon when we arrived at the doctors. It was decided that the wound would have to be stitched. Nobody explained to me what was going to be done and as soon as I was placed on the doctor's couch a rubber mask was clamped to my face which I promptly tried to fight off.

Afterwards my mother always said that the doctor must have had a liquid lunch, in other words too much alcohol to drink with it. Apparently three people had to sit on me while three or four stitches were inserted to hold my cut together and not surprisingly, the resulting ugly scar is still with me.

Soon after that it was time for our annual holiday

to Llanbedrog on the Lleyn Peninsula in North Wales. That year I wasn't allowed to go in the sea as my accident had only happened recently.

During my early childhood, we always went there for our summer holiday. We drove through Bridgnorth, Shrewsbury and onto Chirk with its magnificent castle and grounds on the Welsh border. On one journey the car developed a leak in the roof but fortunately my seaside bucket was handy in which to catch the drops of water. Stains on the fabric lining the roof showed that it had leaked previously.

There was always a picnic on the way. Once it was in a place where there were rocks to lean on while we ate our sandwiches. After packing the remains of the picnic away my mother hit her head badly on one of the rocks. Not a pleasant start to the holiday.

Somewhere on that route we once stopped by the side of a river and watched a weather-beaten old man using a coracle for fishing. He looked up at us and smiled as he guided the coracle into the bank.

'Would your little girl like a ride in the coracle?' he asked my parents in his soft Welsh accent. It was decided that I would, so with the unstable coracle being firmly held so that I didn't fall into the river I gingerly climbed aboard. With his oar he pushed the strange craft away from the bank and it rotated in the swirling eddies of the river. It felt so fragile and so near the water. But the man was experienced at steering the coracle and a few minutes later I was safely on the bank again not realising how lucky I had been to be offered a ride in a coracle.

I didn't know at the time that this form of transport, once used for salmon fishing, was fast dying out and today is only seen in tourist areas. But that was the genuine article and not a tourist attraction so I was fortunate indeed to experience it.

The journey continued along the A5 where at Betwys-y-Coed we often used to stop and admire the rushing Swallow Falls. And then it was into Snowdonia and the wonderful mountains and lakes of which I grew to be so fond in later years.

At the time of which I am writing, when I was a small child, a beach holiday and swimming was the main attraction. We stayed in a house in the village of Llanbedrog where we had all our meals and had a sitting room to ourselves. Each day after breakfast, armed with my bucket and spade and a picnic we descended the steep hill, crossed the main road and went down a narrow tree lined lane with a gurgling stream in a deep gully down one side. Hardly anyone took cars down there as there was nowhere to park. Now I see, looking on Google Earth, there is a car park and like everywhere else, many houses and bungalows have been built. There was a café at the end though, right by the beach and Dad used to go off and buy us ice creams. And once as a real treat I ate an enormous Knickerbocker Glory there.

On the sandy beach there was a line of beach huts and every time we went there for our holiday one was booked for the fortnight. This was our own tiny little house where cups of tea could be made on a primus stove with its characteristic smell; there was shelter if it rained (let's face it this was Wales) and one could change into a bathing costume in privacy. After a swim on cold wet days it was where my mother dried me and tried to get sand off salty wet skin, not a comfortable experience.

Llanbedrog is near to the attractive village of Abersoch, popular with sailing enthusiasts. We went to the chemist there to buy a new bandage for my injured knee. Chemists had a distinctive smell in those days. I seem to remember smells more than what people looked like.

Pwllheli, unmemorable as far as I was concerned and Criccieth are towns along that coast. We visited the castle at Criccieth; sitting with my parents I had a glass of orange juice, while they had cups of tea. A jackdaw suddenly flew onto my head and started clawing at my hair. There was great alarm, not only from me, but from people sitting nearby who rushed to frighten it off. I had shiny blond hair at that time so I suppose, as jackdaws are famed for doing, it was attracted by the bright shininess.

Llanbedrog is where I learned to swim. I also went riding on the beach and up onto the heather covered headland. I remember being very impressed that the woman who owned the riding school was reputed to have thirteen children.

One day when I was seven, we drove to Llanberis and ascended Snowdon on the little mountain train. It was one of those days when the mountain was shrouded in mist. It was just the same many years later when I climbed the mountain with our son and his son. We thought it was quite an achievement to have three generations of the same family on the summit of Snowdon.

Each year we came back from Llanbedrog with a dozen jars of heather honey. My parents bought it from a man who was called Tom Jones, a carpenter and bee keeper. They must have become quite friendly with him and his wife, as we went back every year, for he became 'Uncle Tom', another courtesy uncle and she was 'Auntie Molly'. He made me an intriguing toy which kept me occupied for quite a while. It was a small shallow wooden tray for which he had made several layers of coloured patterns on tracing paper onto which could be placed coloured wooden squares, diamonds and triangles to match the shapes on the tracing paper. What a kind man.

I have happy memories of those holidays at Llanbedrog. We stayed in Mrs Thomas's guest house and the day we left one year she prepared a picnic lunch of corned beef sandwiches for us to eat on our way home. It was decided that we would eat it on Criccieth beach because that was where we would have our last view of the sea for another year. We sat among the large pebbles on the beach with the sea in front of us and the mountains of Snowdonia not far away behind us.

Driving away I would look back wistfully at the

sea. I was already waiting for the following year when the nearer we got I'd be peering ahead ready to shout,

'The sea, the sea,' as soon as I glimpsed it.

One year we went to Eastbourne instead of North Wales. Maybe my parents felt that a holiday on the sunny south coast of England would provide better weather and that we would have golden sands from which to swim.

The journey was sixty miles further than the usual annual trip to North Wales so we set off from home on a Friday afternoon hoping to find somewhere to stay overnight. Several places were tried unsuccessfully en route until finally, late in the evening, we ended up in a hotel in the centre of Slough. The only accommodation they could offer us was a twin-bedded room. My father decided we wouldn't find anywhere else at that time of night so he took the room.

My parents slept together squashed in one of the twin beds and I had the other one all to myself. I doubt if they had a good night and I know I didn't as the roar of traffic outside our window seemed to go on all night. The next morning, somewhat bleary eyed, we set off on the last leg of our journey to Eastbourne.

I don't remember what the weather was like but the beach, certainly at high tide, was a great disappointment being very stony. We stayed in a modest guest house (or was it a superior boarding house?), on Marine Parade just across the road from the beach. Early morning swims were a favourite of my father's and before breakfast I had no choice but to cross the road with him, struggle across the stones and immerse myself in the freezing waters of the English Channel.

Then, blue with cold, it was back for breakfast, sandwiched in between maiden ladies and respectable middle-aged couples to partake of bacon and egg, toast and marmalade in the hotel dining room where hushed whispers were the order of the day.

That is until one of the respectable middle-aged ladies had a fishbone stuck in her throat and disappeared during the evening meal. No one really seemed to notice that she was missing, not even her husband who plodded on with the soggy sprouts, apple crumble and custard, then Jacobs cream crackers, a small square of butter and a hard piece of cheddar cheese which was what answered for a cheese board in those days. It was only over a cup of instant coffee, or was it still the ubiquitous 'Camp' coffee, that he looked around and realised she wasn't at the table any more. He made enquiries as to her whereabouts but by then she was just walking back into the dining room having been discreetly whipped off to Eastbourne hospital to have the offending fishbone removed. She didn't like to make a fuss!

I don't think that was a very successful holiday and we didn't go there again as a family. Some years later my parents holidayed there several times and enjoyed swimming, walking along the Promenade and visiting the theatre. They even thought of retiring there but decided on Devon instead.

Years after my mother had died, when my father was about ninety-five, he was living in a retirement home close to us in Kent. He used to talk about the good times he and my mother had had in Eastbourne so we decided to take him there for a day out. He was having difficulty walking but refused to let us hire a wheel chair for him so he didn't see the delights of the Promenade along which he and my mother had enjoyed walking. His memory was beginning to go and five minutes after we left on the way home he had no idea he had been to the place where he and my mother had spent several enjoyable holidays. That was a bit sad.

*8. Auntie Win and Cousin Mary with
Susie and her Mother*

9. Mary and Susie at Dudley Zoo, 1949

10. Susie and Jeremy in the garden at Northfield

11. Susie on the farm with Sheila, Noffy and Jock

12. Susie with her Mother and Snowy

13. Foxhound puppies in the farmyard

14. Deanie and Marjorie in London

15. Susie aged seven on the summit of Snowdon

16. Riding on Llanbedrog beach

17. Susie with her parents in the garden at Northfield

Chapter Three
Westhill

The Selly Oak Colleges in Birmingham were devoted to the training of missionaries, Sunday School teachers, Youth Workers and, in the case of Westhill College, the training of teachers. They were situated on either side of the Bristol Road about a mile south of Selly Oak and were established in the very early years of the twentieth century; many were influenced by the Cadburys and the Quakers.

Westhill College, established by Quakers in 1907 to train Sunday School teachers, expanded to train youth and community workers. It soon became a pioneering teacher training college following the ideas of Friedrich Froebel (1782-1852). He reformed educational methods, promoting the idea of children learning through play; thus, Kindergartens came about.

The teacher training course was three years, as opposed to the two-year course in non-Froebel colleges, to allow for extra time given to Arts education, Nature Study, Movement and Dance.

There was a school attached to the college and after spending only one year at Rathvilly I became a pupil at that school. I can truly say that it was a most wonderful school and has influenced my whole life and my own teaching in later years.

As well as students from the British Isles there were also Commonwealth students at the college. As I looked out of the classroom window I could sometimes see these students from overseas, often wearing exotic and brightly coloured costumes from their own countries as they walked around the college grounds. Sometimes they would come into school for their teaching practice and thus we heard at first hand of life in various Commonwealth countries, such as what was then known as the Gold Coast (Ghana) and India.

Not all the teachers were English either. There was a German lady, Miss Gurland. She was a tall, thin lady who wore glasses and had a slight German accent. She taught me when I was seven; she never raised her voice to us; her kindness and thoughtful manner were enough to make us want to please her.

I think it is highly likely that Miss Gurland had escaped from Nazi Germany; later when I was at Grammar School I think our German teacher there may also have been a refugee. As children though, we took everything at face value and it was only in later years that I began to wonder what the history of these two ladies might have been. Had they been refugees? Had their families been persecuted by the Nazis or even died in concentration camps? I would never know.

I went to Miss Gurland's funeral many years later. The Anglican church at Bournville was packed, showing that many people had grown to like and be very impressed by this brave and dignified lady.

An Indian lady called Arnie Bartlewalla was another of my teachers; she was known as Miss Arnie. She also lived in historically interesting times, for when she had left her home near Poona, India was still part of the British Empire and when she returned in about 1950 she went back to an independent country.

The school building was divided into two sections with the first three classrooms being on the same level as the main college building, which was further along the drive and to which it was attached with a long corridor. There were several steps down to two more classrooms and the headmistress's office. Her name was Miss Enid Dyer, a lady of medium height; she had grey curly hair and wore glasses. I was shocked once when I came across her once on the floor at the foot of those steps down which she had just fallen. Another adult was helping her to her feet and supporting her as she hobbled off to her office.

The lower part of the school was level with the college playing field where the students played lacrosse. One day one of my classmates called out,

'Oh look, there's been an accident.'

And we all jumped to our feet and followed her gaze to where one of the students had fallen to the ground.

'What's happened, what happened? We all wanted to know as we gathered by the window.

'Calm down children. Go and sit down', our student teacher replied. This was one of the occasions when one of the students was doing her teaching practice in our classroom. While trying to restore normality to the classroom we could see that she too was wondering what had happened to one of her friends. Then we all watched as the young female student who had fallen and hurt her leg was being carried off the field by two other students.

On the other side of the building was a lawn, a pond and a copse next to the main Bristol Road, whilst adjacent to it was a large playground with a collection of climbing frames and swings at the far end.

I must return to my early days at Westhill School when I joined the class that was called Transition. I had missed out on the Kindergarten class as I had spent my first school year at Rathvilly. I also missed a whole term of school during that first year at Westhill due to having measles very badly followed by a serious ear infection. The timing of my illness pre-dated the use of anti-biotics and the complications of an ear infection were much worse than they would be today.

I remember being taken to see a specialist and having an X-ray. It had been explained to me that it wouldn't hurt and was just like having a photograph taken and so I wasn't afraid and found the process fascinating unlike a small boy in the waiting room who was screaming loudly. What a shame that no one had taken the trouble to explain the process to him as it had been explained to me.

Afterwards I was fascinated to see that the X-ray showed a head full of teeth that would emerge in the next few years. The specialist recommended a mastoid operation which I believe would have left me with a small hole behind my ear and precluded me from swimming and putting my head underwater in the future.

My mother was keen to find out if there was an alternative. She took me to see a Naturopath who recommended that I should gargle with diluted lemon juice and eat a diet high in fruit, salads and vegetables. When I was taken back to see the specialist about six weeks later he was amazed at the improvement in my condition. The operation was no longer necessary. I owe a lot to my mother's determination to find and follow through an alternative way. The specialist was loath to admit that alternative medicine had won the day. The 'Food Reform Diet' and Vegetarianism were labelled as cranky in those days and if you ate wholemeal bread you were very odd. How different it is today.

So eventually I was restored to health but missing so much school at such a crucial time came at a cost, especially to the development of my mathematical ability. This was not helped either during the ensuing years when my father, a very able mathematician, always wanted to work out my homework problems very quickly in his way, before starting to understand the methods I had been taught. While he quickly solved my equations and fractions I was left feeling even more stupid. I don't suppose he had any idea that he was undermining my confidence for years to come.

However, I got there in the end and was rather pleased when, while I was still a very young teacher, I had a school leaver observing my class for a week or so. He had been studying A Level Maths. We both did the end of term maths test that had been set for my pupils and not only did I complete it more quickly than he did but I made fewer mistakes. Not too bad, I thought to myself.

I remember little of that first year at Westhill except the catastrophe I caused due to me being such a wilful child.

Froebel education was very hands on, very child centred and in that class we had a pretend shop. In addition to items to 'sell' which we put out on a table there were shelves on the table where we could display further items.

At that time every primary school child had a free third of a pint bottle of milk each day at morning play time. We could display them in our shop but were given a strong warning only to put a very small number of bottles of milk on the shelves in case they toppled over.

You have probably guessed by now what happened. This wilful child decided she knew best and put too many bottles on the shelves and the whole lot came crashing down. I remember a sea of milk and broken glass on the brown linoleum floor of the classroom. I don't remember a teacher shouting at me, I don't remember being told off but surely, I must have been admonished. Whatever do you do when you have a classful of six-year olds, a sea of milk rapidly spreading over the floor and, most dangerous of all, a quantity of broken glass lying around? In my teaching career, many years later, I was spared that sort of disaster, thank goodness. But when I caused the Milk Disaster 'Miss' must have been less than pleased!

The following year I was in Miss Gurland's class. Her classroom was at the side of the building where a long window overlooked the Headmistress's garden. On the 5th December when we were almost ready to go home she said,

'I want you all to leave a shoe on the windowsill this afternoon before you go.'

'Why do you want us to do that Miss?'

'It's a secret. You'll find out in the morning.'

She wouldn't tell us the reason but dismissed us with a mysterious smile on her face.

When we returned the next morning we were surprised to see that all the shoes were filled with nuts, apples and oranges.

'Good morning children,' she greeted us and looked around at our happy faces. When we were sitting at our desks she said,

'I can see that you are all smiling at my surprise. Now I can tell you that this is a German custom. In Germany the children are told that St Nicholas is coming during the night so they must leave a shoe out. The good children will find next morning that he has put fruit and nuts in their shoes.'

Wasn't that a delightful way to introduce us to the

customs of another country.

That classroom had a small additional room to one side which came in very useful when we were learning about cavemen. It became our darkened 'cave' and into it went our charcoal drawings of prehistoric animals and people, and the clay lamps we had made.

When visiting caves in France some years ago the guide took us through narrow passageways and pointed out the paintings of the wild animals that the cave men had hunted thousands of years ago. It was almost incomprehensible to visualise how a prehistoric man had held the picture in his head of the animal he had hunted and then transferred that image to the rock wall in front of us. The guide shone his torch beam at the pictures but prehistoric man must have had a flickering taper or a burning stick as his light.

At Westhill music and dance were important parts of our education and across a wide corridor from Miss Gurland's classroom was the large room used for the Kindergarten class. That was where we sat cross legged on the cold brown lino and had our music lessons. Miss Hunter, with a long face and brown hair pulled back into a bun, was our teacher. I don't remember many of the songs we were taught but 'The Bailiff's Daughter from Islington' sticks in my mind and of course, carols at Christmas.

Christmas was a very special time at Westhill. We had all joined in with making the Christmas cake, helping to add the ingredients and giving it all a good stir. At that time we were still in the post-war era of rationing and I remember that dried egg powder was added to the other ingredients.

The Christmas concert, to which parents were invited, took place in the beautiful College Common Room with its highly-polished parquet floor and tall, white pillars supporting the ceiling. A huge Christmas tree had been placed at one side of the room and each child in turn was, with an adult's guiding hand, allowed to light a real candle on the tree. It was magic. Can my memory really serve me correctly here? In these days of great attention being paid to Health and Safety this would never happen. I can vividly recall when it was my turn to light a candle. What a thrill it was.

Then, when the lights had been turned down all the children, sitting cross-legged on the floor started to sing carols.

Little Jesus, sweetly sleep, do not stir.
We will lend a coat of fur.
We will rock you, rock you, rock you
We will rock you, rock you, rock you
See the fur to keep you warm,
Snugly round your tiny form.

The following September, I moved up the school and down the steps to the next class which was Miss Arnie's class. Here amongst other topics we learnt something about India. We performed a play and we learned how to greet people with our hands clasped in front of us and to give a slight bow. We also continued with our Maths, English, Nature Study, Drama, Art, PE and Music.

One-day my mother invited Miss Arnie to have tea with us at our house in Northfield and I have a lovely memory of her standing at the top of the drive with her beautiful pink sari wafting around her in the breeze as she waved goodbye. She went back to India soon afterwards and this had been a farewell visit.

I was an avid reader and having moved into the upper part of the school had access to the long rows of bookshelves in the corridor that ran alongside the classrooms. I worked my way enthusiastically through all Arthur Ransome's Swallows and Amazon books about the family of four children who went on holiday to the Lake District and were allowed to go sailing. There was book after book of their adventures with the two Blackett girls they had met and then later I read 'We didn't Mean to go to Sea' about how, when they were in East Anglia, their boat somehow became cast adrift and they ended up sailing to Holland.

We also had plenty of books at home and I enjoyed reading those that my mother had kept from her childhood. One such book that I found fascinating was 'The Queen's Gift Book', which was a thick pale blue tome. In 1915 during the First World War, Hodder and Stoughton, at the suggestion of Queen Mary, wife of King George the fifth, had published this book to raise funds for wounded soldiers. The book sold for 2s 6d and the proceeds went to Queen Mary's Convalescent Auxiliary Hospitals for Soldiers and

Sailors who had lost their limbs in the War. There were contributions from JM Barrie, Joseph Conrad, Jerome K Jerome and Sir Arthur Conan Doyle, with illustrations by Arthur Rackham, W. Heath Robinson and other artists.

When I was reading it the book already seemed old and well-thumbed and yet it was less than forty years since it had been published during the First World War and now there had been yet another world war and Queen Mary was still alive. She died in 1953 at the age of eighty-five.

Another book, with a green cover and an attractive gold design, that had belonged to my mother was Louisa M. Allcot's 'Little Women'. I still have that book and taking it down from my bookshelf and reading the inscription inside I see that it was given to her by her friend Marjorie Cleave in April 1916. It was a present for my mother for her thirteenth birthday over a hundred years ago.

I met Marjorie many years later when she was living in Bedford with her husband Dan. Their romance soon after the First World War had a stormy journey, as he was sent to Australia after she became pregnant when they were still both in their teens. He returned eventually and they married and had several more children. As a child, I found it quite mystifying when I overheard my father saying,

'Dan only had to hang his coat on the bedpost for her to have another baby'.

I wondered much later if there could have been a

touch of irony here when he and my mother had failed even to conceive one baby.

When I was about ten we visited them where they were living in Bedford and Dan took us out on the River Ouse in his motor boat. When we arrived back to its mooring place we climbed up the steps to the quay as Dan tidied up the boat before leaving it. My father was carrying a petrol can which he somehow managed to drop and it landed on Dan's head making a small cut. We all realised it had hurt Dan considerably as he sat in the boat with his head bowed until he felt able to climb the ladder and join us on the quayside. A very unfortunate incident.

Other books I enjoyed were the 'Just So Stories' by Rudyard Kipling, 'Black Beauty' by Anna Sewell, 'What Katy Did' by Susan Coolidge and other books written by Louisa M Alcott. When I was younger I read about the 'Flopsy Bunnies' and all the other delightful creatures in the Beatrix Potter Books. I had all the Little Grey Rabbit books by Alison Uttley and read about the adventures of the Squirrel, the Hare and the Little Grey Rabbit. A. A. Milne's stories about Winnie the Pooh, Piglet, Eeyore, Rabbit, Kanga and Roo kept me amused for hours. Some people can be scathing about the anthropomorphism in such books but it cannot be denied that attributing human traits and emotions to animals and indeed even plants is very popular with children. Not only do we see it here with the above-mentioned books but long-ago programmes on television such as the 'Plant Pot Men' (remember

'Weed?') delighted many children.

The Froebel education that Westhill provided gave me a great awareness of the world around me. Subjects were not chopped up into unrelated areas but were inter-linked, a practice that I and most other teachers followed later when I was teaching Junior aged children. That was a process known as being 'Project Based'. For instance, deciding to have a project on Water you would see how Geography, History, Science, Maths and Art could be brought into it. Learning is much more fun with this approach.

One Autumn I walked with the rest of my class along the Bristol Road to the grounds of the Manor House in which Dame Elizabeth Cadbury lived. I remember seeing her once, perhaps at a garden party or fete in the grounds of the Manor House, a dignified, old lady in her mid-nineties at the time; when she died in 1951 she was ninety-seven.

She was an English philanthropist, had been awarded the DBE and was the wife of George Cadbury. Throughout her life she campaigned for the education and welfare of women and children and worked energetically to provide medical inspections in schools. She was a Liberal, became a Birmingham City councillor and was a magistrate among her many other activities. Later the Manor House became a Hall of Residence for the University of Birmingham.

Our visit was a wonderful opportunity to be able to see the grounds of her house and walk around the large lake. We noted the ripples on the water and ducks and moorhens swimming there. We looked at the vegetation surrounding the lake, the reeds, the rosebay willow herb, the trees changing colour and some late flowers. A gardener was sweeping up fallen leaves and smoke from a bonfire was drifting up into the sky and swirling away among the branches of the trees. It was a typical misty Autumn morning and we were being trained to be observant.

In the following days, back at school we painted what we had seen by the lake, including the smoke swirling round the trees. We wrote a poem about the lake and its surroundings in Autumn and we looked up details of the flora and fauna we had come across. That made a lasting impression on me, still vivid after nearly seventy years.

We had a pond in the school grounds which provided inspiration for nature study; in the spring there were frogs and tadpoles and other water creatures there. We explored the college grounds and went along the lime walk where the heavily scented blossom attracted bees.

Close to the classrooms were the playing fields where the students played lacrosse. Some of the them did their teaching practice in the school and I remember getting into trouble for being cheeky with one young lady student who sent me to stand outside the Headmistress's door as I was such a pest. She was a friendly student though and my misdemeanours did not prevent her from drawing an excellent picture in my autograph book of Winnie the Pooh getting stuck in the rabbit hole when he had eaten too much honey and condensed milk while visiting Rabbit.

Early in 1952 we moved from the house in Northfield back to Weoley Hill which, like the first home I had lived in, was on Bournville Village Trust land. All the houses were on plots surrounded by beech hedges and they all had good sized gardens. From this house I was able to walk down the hill to school at Westhill. A walk which in the spring was particularly delightful as it was under flowering cherry trees.

I walked home too, often with my friend Roberta. By now I was ten and sometimes a little group of us would leave the school by the back way, the footpath that led onto Fox Hill. At the bottom of the hill was the post office that was also a general store and sold sweets. Sweets were still more or less forbidden at home, it being the days when the rare Mars Bar would be cut into thin slices and lasted a week. Nevertheless, out of sight of my mother, I would sometimes go down to the post office with my friends and invest a few pennies of my pocket money in the sort of rubbish like sherbet fizzes and black jacks that seemed good value for money at the time.

One day, with a handful of these illicit sweets, I was walking up the hill with my friends when my mother turned up in the car to collect me. Quickly pushing the forbidden goodies into someone else's welcoming hands, I climbed into the car hoping my mother hadn't cottoned on to what I was doing. I think I got away with my guilty secret that time. I think her eyes were on the road and not on me or she would soon have wondered why I had such a red face.

When I was in the penultimate year at Westhill the headmistress, Miss Enid Dyer, came into our classroom one cold, wet February day when the windows were steamed up with condensation. Her eyes were full of tears. We all stopped what we were doing and looked at her in alarm.

'The King has died,' she said.

I think the fact that here was a grown up, and a teacher at that, who was almost crying in front of us, left a more lasting impression than the news she had come to impart.

In the following days the newspapers were full of stories of how the young Queen Elizabeth had hurriedly come back from Kenya. We saw pictures of her, her mother and sister deeply veiled in black at the funeral. We didn't have a television in those days so if we wanted to see the news we went to the cinema where we could see it all on a Pathé newsreel after the main film.

My father was on the office staff at H.W. Wards machine tool factory in Selly Oak and occasionally I went there with him on a Saturday morning. There within the hallowed atmosphere of his office were drawing boards and very sharp pencils, coloured crayons and an office chair with a swivelling seat where I would sit for a while drawing and no doubt breaking some of those very sharp points. Dad wouldn't be there for long as he didn't work on Saturdays. As we left we'd walk through the factory where I saw row after row of huge lathes, curls of metal from the machining process on the floor underneath them. All-pervading was the distinctive smell of machine tool oil.

On June 2nd, 1953, we went to the home of George and Peggy Hooson for the day to view the Coronation on their television. George was the son of the man who played the cello with my father and was a colleague of his at the factory in Selly Oak.

Coronation Day was a momentous occasion; about a dozen people crowded round the small screen. Mrs Hooson provided a delicious running buffet of sandwiches and sausage rolls. All over the country people were making a day of it and gathering together with friends and neighbours.

The icing on the cake was the news that came in on the morning of the Coronation that Edmund Hillary and Sherpa Tensing had conquered Everest. Later, when I was at Grammar School the whole school went to see the film of this amazing feat. Nowadays climbing Everest is commonplace.

At the time of the Coronation everybody felt very patriotic and immensely proud of our young Queen. People had slept out overnight in the Mall to be assured of a good viewpoint for the procession. It was a damp morning and plastic pakamacs were much in evidence but nothing could dampen the enthusiasm of the crowd. The Queen of Tonga won everybody's hearts when, despite the rain, she insisted on having the hood of her carriage down so she could see and be seen. She was a very jolly sight on a wet day.

During the summer there were street parties and fancy-dress parades. I and my friends dressed patriotically in red, white and blue costumes of some sort or another for a party at the tennis club down the road. We were given a Coronation mug and a flat tin of chocolate.

The years at Westhill passed happily although I did come in for a certain amount of bullying from a girl called Hazel. But I didn't even dream of telling my parents about it and when my mother noticed a dirty mark on the back of my jumper resulting from a playground scuffle, I merely told her I'd rubbed it on a tree in the garden. Having said earlier that I had given up lying was obviously an untruth in itself. Well rules are made to be bent but the idea of telling tales seemed to be abhorrent to me at the time.

Hazel's bullying was part of the reason that I chose not to go to the local grammar school at Kings Norton; she was going there. I wanted a fresh start away from her, so I chose to go to George Dixon Grammar School. Also my friend Roberta would be going there the following year. As it turned out it was an excellent choice because of what happened in 1956 but that story must come later.

Chapter Four
Friends and Relations

As an only child, my small world at first consisted of my parents and me and the springer spaniel with which they had come back from Cornwall before the war.

I suppose my mother's older sister was the first family member of whom I became aware. Auntie Glad, tall, overpowering and with a deep, booming voice was quite daunting to a small child. She had a heart of gold but she filled me with awe not admiration.

When I was three I was sent to stay with her for three months whilst my mother was recovering from a hysterectomy. In those days, the recovery period was a full three months so my sojourn with Auntie Glad seemed endless. She must have been about fifty so I don't suppose it was particularly easy having a three-year-old to stay for that length of time. Her daughter, my cousin Phil, was in her early twenties then, still living at home before she was married. Aunty Glad's husband, Uncle Len, was there too but both he and Phil went off to work in Birmingham each morning, catching the train into town from the station at Olton at the end of the road and I was left with Auntie Glad all day. I was very young and I don't remember much of the visit but I do remember that Auntie Glad had a lovely singing voice and at night when I had been put to bed she sang 'Christopher Robin is saying his prayers' to me.

> Little boy kneels at the foot of his bed
> Droops on his little hands, little gold head

and further on

> If I open my eyes just a little bit more
> I can see Nanny's dressing gown on the door.

I really could visualise that child kneeling by his bed trying to remember to ask God to bless his mother and father and finally, 'God bless me', he said.

They had a dog called Peggy, a grey spotted dog of indeterminate breed. I seem to remember that Peggy didn't like me much and possibly tried to nip me, or maybe it was the other way around and I didn't like Peggy much and tormented her but anyway I used to be lifted up to sit on a built-in green painted sideboard with a brown lino top that was situated at the side of the kitchen. Once sitting on it I was out of harm's way. From there I had an unobstructed view of the kitchen with its black leaded range and oil-cloth covered large kitchen table where meals were eaten. Windows at the side overlooked a passageway between that house and the neighbouring one. Betty lived there, a young lady who didn't mind entertaining a small child. We used to sit on her lawn cutting up windfall apples. She was very friendly. Surely at three years of age I wasn't doing the cutting?

From my viewpoint on the sideboard I could see through to the small scullery to where there was a sink and the huge mangle. There must have been a gas stove too for I remember the pervading smell of potato peelings being boiled up with hen food for the chickens that Uncle Len kept in the back garden. From the scullery, a passage way led to the back door. As well as the smell of chicken food being boiled up there was a pervading feeling of damp.

There were two other rooms downstairs, a very pleasant sitting room with doors that could open onto the garden but I don't ever remember seeing them open. There were three china ducks flying across the wall. They never seemed to get anywhere.

And there was a front room which later Phil and her husband Terry had as their sitting room when they were first married, before they had their own home.

My lengthy stay with Auntie Glad came to an end and my mother came to take me home. Poor Auntie was mortified when, on seeing my mother, I burst into tears. Auntie wanted to show that I had been happy to stay with her but I cried with relief at seeing my mother again.

I was Phil's bridesmaid when she was married in 1951. I wore a long pink dress that had a pretty matching bonnet which lined with white velvet and tied with pink satin ribbons. Tiny pink hyacinth flowers were sewn onto the side of it.

I was not popular when I trod on Phil's veil as she

and Terry walked down the aisle. She had to clutch at her head to stop the veil and head dress falling off. I had literally put my foot in it.

Sadly, only six years later Phil was widowed when Terry died of TB. A year or so before Terry's sad demise they started to foster Peggy, a four-year-old girl. Auntie Glad berated Peggy for not crying when Terry died but my mother remembered the frightened little girl who was terrified that she would have to leave Phil. But she stayed with her and when Auntie Glad and Uncle Len moved to Bournemouth on his retirement Phil and Peggy moved to live there too.

When I was staying with Auntie Glad I think I had sensed an atmosphere in the house that was different from my own home and I certainly became more aware of it as I grew older. Auntie and Uncle were always bickering, always trying to belittle each other, always sensing, rightly or wrongly that they had been slighted. Auntie was the dominant one in the partnership and Uncle resented it. She was a very capable woman and when Len had returned from fighting in the First World War, and during the dreadful unemployment afterwards, she encouraged him to study for the Civil Service exams. He passed them and thus a good career in the Civil Service was assured. He worked in the Income Tax office in Birmingham and much later, when I was a student, he obtained a job for me there during the summer vacation.

Maybe Uncle Len resented the fact that Auntie Glad had moulded his future. He might have been just as happy in some humdrum job. I got on all right with him but he was a man of few words and usually had a cigarette attached to his lips. At that time, most men smoked. I suppose it became a habit when they were stuck in the trenches during WW1 as Uncle Len had been.

It wasn't until years later that I came to understand Auntie Glad properly. Her mother, Susie Priddey, had been born in New York in 1869 while her father was a railway clerk on one of the American railways forging its way across the United States. Three years earlier a brother had been born in Erie City, Pennsylvania so the family must have moved around a bit. Three years before that their daughter Elizabeth was born in Upton-on Severn, Worcestershire in England. Elizabeth became known as Lizzie to her family, Great Aunt Lizzie to me later, and as I have mentioned, was still alive as a very old lady when I was a small child, living in a nursing home somewhere in Birmingham.

I remember she was in a room full of aged ladies sitting around waiting for death when I went to see her with my mother. My recently acquired knowledge of where babies came from must have been uppermost in my mind because apparently, in a loud voice, I asked her if she had a baby in her tummy. I can imagine now the shocked silence when a maiden lady of over eighty was confronted by a small girl asking her that question. Now I can feel for my poor mother's embarrassment too.

In her younger years, Auntie Lizzie, as she was to

my mother, had been a great support to her sister Susie's family. Susie's marriage had not been a happy one and her husband, Frederic Sharp, was a philanderer. Although he was still around at the time of the 1911 census, living at the family home in Smallheath, Birmingham, I think his links with the family were already tenuous. My mother told me of times when she was very young when she would have to accompany her mother on the search for her husband to demand money for the family's upkeep. My mother found this very distressing and told me that it and the fact that her father had left home had upset her so much that she was unable to walk for a while.

But Auntie Lizzy, who had become a successful business woman, stepped in to help. She was in residence at the family home on the night of the census in 1911 which enabled me to find out that the Priddey family came from Upton-on-Severn in Worcestershire.

But money continued to be a problem, so much so that Auntie Glad had to leave school at fourteen and go out to work to help support the family and presumably this also applied to her twin brother. Cyril and Gladys, born in 1894 were one of two sets of twins born in that family. The second set, Douglas and Philip, were born in 1898. Poor Susie must really have had her hands full. Just think of getting one baby ready to go out, let alone two sets of twins.

When Susie was again expecting a baby in 1903 she must have wondered if another set of twins would arrive. I can imagine her relief when on Easter Sunday

1903, during a snowstorm, just a single baby, my mother, Marjorie, arrived. Not that they ever called her Marjorie for she became known as 'Baby Darling'. Before long that was shortened to Bab and to that side of the family Bab she remained, even being known as Auntie Bab when the next generation came along.

It was one thing being known as 'Baby Darling' by her adoring siblings when she was very small but quite another being the youngest in a domineering set of brothers and a sister as she became an adult. And there was a certain amount of resentment towards her later from her sister because when she left school there was now enough money to enable her to continue her education at Art College. Eventually she married a man with greater ambitions than Uncle Len and so financially had a more comfortable life. It's not surprising that Gladys felt her little sister was having a better deal in life.

In 1914 when the First World War started, Cyril, aged twenty, enlisted in the army and before long his two younger brothers, Douglas and Philip, also joined up. Susie had three boys fighting in France and when the telegrams started coming to many houses along the street her heart must have been in her mouth dreading that the telegram boy would come to her home.

In November 1917, a telegram did arrive telling her that Philip, aged nineteen, had been killed at Ypres. He was a driver in the Royal Field Artillery and is buried in the Tyne Cot Cemetery. I still have the letter his commanding officer sent to Susie notifying her of his death. A notification that thousands of mothers in Birmingham and elsewhere, received. Life for that family and for hundreds of other families, was never the same again. My mother used to say that it was her favourite brother that had been killed.

1917 was the year my parents met. Dad's father, James Williams, had died that year and Mum had lost her favourite brother, Philip, so they had both lost a family member. It was the start of an enduring and loving relationship which lasted until my mother died in 1981.

I have already said that I found Auntie Glad overpowering. It seemed that she was very confident and approached life from a strong position but I wonder if that was perhaps not the case. Maybe she too had been affected by her father's desertion of the family and lacked security. I found it poignant that she had to push herself forward at the time of my marriage by announcing to people,

'I'm the Bride's Aunt you know', in case she should be overlooked. I hope that doesn't sound unkind. She just wanted to be part of the action, to be noticed. When I look back at the photo of my christening when both she and Auntie Sylvia were my godmothers I see that she was the one holding the baby.

Her twin brother Cyril was also a very domineering person. Pleasant and decisive but always absolutely sure he was right. On more than one occasion he said,

'I *know* I'm right', should there be any doubt on the matter under discussion.

He was a physical training instructor during WW1 and after the war became a Physical Education teacher at King Edward High School, at that time situated in New Street in Birmingham. Later he held the same position at King Edward School at Five Ways in Birmingham.

He fell in love with Nora. She was beautiful and an accomplished dancer. Not until later did Cyril discover why he had not been introduced to her mother. Cyril and Nora were married in 1922 and the following year a son, Eric, was born to them.

My mother said even when Eric was a small child Nora seemed strangely clumsy with him. As the years went on the clumsiness got worse and her movements became uncontrollable. Most of the china in the house was smashed and Cyril had to take over the running of the home. Tragically she was diagnosed with the incurable Huntington's Chorea which she had inherited from her mother. This was the secret her family had been hiding from Cyril.

Eric became a sailor during the Second World War when he was a signalman in the Royal Navy. When he had flu soon after the war had ended he came to stay with us when we were living in Northfield as his mother would not have been able to look after him. By this time her movements were so erratic that sadly she had knocked most of her teeth out.

In the early 1950s Eric married Joan but

unfortunately later he also developed the disease.

Poor Norah, I remember seeing her when I was a child and probably found her rather frightening. Eventually she became hospitalised and the person who had been the beautiful girl that Cyril had married died in 1960.

Uncle Douglas, whose twin brother had been killed at Ypres in 1917 and who was one of Susie Sharp's second set of twins, was not quite so domineering as his older siblings but one had a feeling of never quite knowing how you stood with him. He was an impatient man who felt it was his right to have his wife wait on him. He could be very charming but I wasn't sure how genuine it was. He was the only one of Susie's children who became divorced; I never knew his first wife or daughter.

His second wife, Louise, was the most delightful person you could possibly meet. She was a primary school teacher and was clever, artistic and a very good cook. Despite being a very busy lady who was teaching full time in a local school as well as running her own home and bringing up their son Philip, she always welcomed guests to her home and nothing was too much trouble. She organised the most wonderful children's Hallowe'en parties where she dressed up as a witch and decorated the house with spooky objects.

I used to go and stay in their home from time to time and she always made such a fuss of me, making sure I had warm fluffy towels for my bath and scented talcum powder. She was a very dear lady and I'm sure she influenced my choice of career.

Their son Philip was always rather full of himself, encouraged by his father and, it must be admitted, a bit spoilt by his mother. Like the rest of the family though he was in his element when he was in a position of authority and made a wonderful usher at our wedding. I was never quite sure why he ended up in Papua New Guinea, probably he found a role for himself in telling the people there how to organise their lives. I expect he was very good at it. He died in 2007.

On my father's side of the family there was just his elder brother, two siblings having died in infancy. Uncle Percy, Percy James Williams, was two years older than my father and one of my favourite uncles. He was very approachable and had a round face, twinkly eyes and a cheeky grin. A little joke of his, not done when I was very young though, was to shake hands with a very strong grip to see who would give up first. He was always prepared to listen to me and never treated me like a mere child.

Like my mother's brothers he'd also fought in the First World War when he'd been a pilot in the Royal Flying Corps. Flying was in its infancy and many pilots were killed in training as well as in battle in the skies. The average life expectancy for an Allied pilot then was just eleven days. They took to the skies in planes that were rickety frames of plywood covered in flammable fabric next to tanks of highly combustible fuel.

Uncle Percy crashed twice and finally he was invalided out of the Royal Flying Corps but the effects of his flying exploits lasted for many years. Today we would call it post-traumatic stress disorder but then it was just called nightmares.

During WW2, he and his wife moved out of Birmingham to escape the bombing. He had married Marjorie Priscilla Toney in 1923 and she was known as Madge, Auntie Madge to me. They left Birmingham to avoid the bombing during WW2 and lived for a while with his cousin Win and her family in her house at Wood End near the village of Tanworth-in-Arden in Warwickshire. Later they found a delightful cottage to rent just along the road. It was conveniently placed near the station so that Uncle could still reach his work in Birmingham where he was a partner in a factory that made aluminium saucepans among other things.

Old Forge Cottage, with its wooden beams and uneven floors, had originally been a forge and the forge itself at one end of the cottage was quite unchanged. This was the place where people had brought their horses to be shod, the wide doors opening onto the road.

The main living room had an old range in it and Auntie Madge had brightly polished horse brasses hanging from the bressummer above the range. I have some of these now in my cottage in France. In the centre of the room was a large dining table and on one side of the room next to the window with leaded glass panes she had a polished antique oak dresser where lovely flower arrangements and old china plates were displayed. Auntie's homes were immaculate. From this room, a doorway led into a small sitting room in which was a fireplace where Uncle had log fires. The huge fires in the small room made it far too hot and often the windows would have to be opened even in the winter.

After the sumptuous meals that Auntie served she and my mother would do the washing up while I, as a small child, dozed on the sofa in the sitting room listening with half an ear to Uncle and my father discussing stocks and shares and consulting the pink Financial Times. After that there would often be a walk round the county lanes and then back for tea before we drove home along moonlit lanes where rabbits, dazzled by the car headlights, froze in fear in the road.

The cottage had a large garden where Uncle grew vegetables and Auntie grew flowers and where there was what Auntie called her 'cobblestone patch' which was a small paved sitting area where a vine with tiny, tart grapes clung to the wall. At the end of the garden was an orchard with prolific plum trees. In the centre of the lawn was a large natural pond that had frogs, frogspawn and newts in it, dragon flies flying over it and bull rushes growing around it. It was a natural dew pond and in the days before the cottage garden was gentrified, farm animals came to drink from it.

Along the back of the cottage an extension had been built which held a kitchen, a bathroom and a toilet and a passageway that led to the outside. At the other end of the kitchen was the north-facing dairy, a wonderfully cool room with a stone floor and shelves where stone slabs kept food cold. This was in pre-refrigerator days.

My cousin Mary lived with her parents Win and Bill Evans just along the lane at Hardwick House. When Win had inherited it from her mother, Annie, it had been called Daffodil Farm but in memory of the place where her Etherington ancestors had come from near Alcester, she renamed it Hardwick House. It was here that Uncle Percy and Auntie Madge had lived temporarily before they found Old Forge Cottage.

Mary and I had a lot of fun together as children. We were both only children, she is just a year older than I am and we enjoyed each other's company. Now well over seventy years later we still are very comfortable talking to each other although, as she lives in the far north of Scotland and I live in the south of England, it is some years since we last met, but we're glad to be able to have long conversations on the phone when we re-live memories of those distant days when we visited Auntie's Madge's cottage and played in the garden or amused ourselves back at Mary's home.

There was land at Hardwick House and tomatoes were grown in the greenhouses there. And there was a large pantechnicon which was seeing out its days in a quiet corner and we played in that. Mary told me that it was the lorry in which Auntie Madge and Uncle Percy's furniture was moved out of Birmingham when they went to live at Wood End.

Auntie Madge's cottage was just along the lane and sometimes we swam in the pond in her garden.

Auntie's house was spotlessly clean and yet when we came in covered in mud from the pond she didn't seem to turn a hair as we washed the mud off our bodies in her pristine bathroom. In the late summer, we feasted on the ripe plums from her orchard and came out covered in spots from midge bites. They had been feasting on us while we feasted on the plums.

Often at Christmas and on other occasions during the year the grown-ups would get together; my parents, Mary's parents and Auntie Madge and Uncle Percy who had no children of their own.

The grown-ups would chatter in the sitting room while Mary and I lay on the carpet in front of the range in the dining room enjoying ourselves with the crayons and colouring books that Uncle Percy had bought for us.

He was always very generous and as we left to go home he could be counted on to dig his hand into his pocket and produce a florin.

With a twinkle in his eye, he'd say,

'Would you like to buy yourself an ice cream?'

'Oh, yes please Uncle, thank you!'

Uncle Percy's affable manner was very much in contrast to Mary's father, a gruff and difficult person, not known for showing her any affection. Mary told me in later years he never showed her any fondness.

'I was very envious of your home life,' she said to me once. 'Your parents seemed so normal!'

Mary was always aware that there was some mystery regarding her mother's parentage but her mother wouldn't talk about it. Her grandmother was Annie Etherington and, unknown to Mary until much later, her mother Win, had been Annie's illegitimate child.

My father lived for part of his childhood with his grandparents, George and Amelia Etherington, at Rushbrook Farm near Tanworth-in Arden. The story went that he'd been sent out to live there because he was weak but since he lived to the ripe old age of ninety-eight I rather doubt that. I think he was sent there because he was hyperactive.

This fits with stories he told me of returning after the three-mile walk back from school, as a small boy, finding Grandma had not yet returned from market and spending a happy half hour or so chasing the hens round the farm yard. He also told me how he used to be sent to fetch the carthorses in from the fields, huge great beasts and him a skinny little seven-year-old.

In the winter, to avoid that long walk twice a day in bad weather, he lived during the week in his Auntie Annie's cottage by the village green in Tanworth. He was very fond of his cousin Win and they went to the village school together. This was where he witnessed the cruelty of the children who mocked Win for being illegitimate. She found this very hurtful and would never talk about it; hence she kept her secret and it was only after her death that Auntie Madge told Mary the truth about Win's birth.

Once we went to stay with Auntie Madge on our own. By that time Mary's parents had moved away from Hardwick House and had gone to live in Solihull. Our stay at the cottage was not entirely successful mainly because of the bed we had to share. Neither of us was used to sharing a bed and in this case the bed was on a sloping floor and we kept rolling into each other. Auntie Madge was faced with two tearful little girls feeling homesick. She said we could go home the next day if we wanted to but I can't remember if we did or not. In the light of day, we probably realised that we were having too good a time to go home early.

We didn't see as much of each other as we grew older and developed our own circle of friends near to our own homes. Mary subsequently met and married a dear man called Alan who tragically died of cancer at the early age of forty-eight.

Later Uncle Percy and Auntie Madge had a rather splendid house called White Gables, built for them nearer to Tanworth village. I went to stay with them there one summer when my parents went on holiday during term time. I enjoyed the morning walk along country lanes to the station at Wood End and the train journey into Birmingham to Grammar School. Auntie's house, just like the cottage, was immaculate and the food she provided was very generous. They were still living there when I was married and Uncle gave me a wonderful set of saucepans made in his factory for a wedding present.

When I was a little girl Dad took me to see his Uncle Tom who was his mother's brother and brother to Annie Etherington. Uncle Tom's pig had just given birth to thirteen baby piglets. He was a full-time farmer with cows, pigs, a shire horse, hens and a huge greenhouse for tomatoes and he had a large vegetable garden too. He and his wife, clothes protected with durable sacking aprons, were hard working and almost self-sufficient. My father said that Thomas's father George had drunk two fortunes away and was reduced to being a tenant farmer. He would chase his wife and children round the fields when he was drunk. Another story is of George coming home drunk, travelling with the pony and trap and falling asleep. But all was well as the pony knew the way home. My mother said that when he was an old man George was the mildest of men, very different from his younger years.

Dad's Uncle Tom and his wife had an open range for cooking, with a kettle hanging over the fire and half a salted pig hanging from hooks on the ceiling.

There was no electricity, gas or mains water; a pump outside the back door delivered water from a well. The toilet, an earth privy, was down the garden.

This is the sort of organic, self-sufficient life style that some people crave today.

'Back to the land,' they urge.

It may be wonderful to grow your own food and rear your own animals but it's not an easy life and you can't pop off on holiday to Spain or wherever; your animals and land need you all the time. And, by the way, the life I've been describing on Tom Etherington's farm wasn't pre-war. That's what it was like in the 1950s.

Later the farm was sold and no doubt the next owner brought it into the twentieth century with mains water, electricity and indoor plumbing. So Dad's Uncle Tom and his life style became part of history; a life style that some people regret has passed.

We only have to go back a few generations to find that many of us have our roots in the land. I've been writing here about the family I was adopted into but my natural family too were farmers and agricultural labourers in Warwickshire, Northamptonshire and on the Welsh Borders.

I said that Uncle Percy was a favourite uncle; another one was Uncle Ken who wasn't really an uncle at all. He and his wife, Auntie Sylvia, were my godparents and I was very fond of them indeed.

Auntie Sylvia and my mother had worked together at the First Aid Post during the war. They lived near to us, not far from Bournville and had three adopted children. While the children were still quite young they moved to live in a cottage on the edge of the Forest of Dean, a few miles from Monmouth. Their white stone cottage had a few small fields which were surrounded by the forest and had a very pretty, sloping garden bounded by a hedge. A stream gurgled down the hillside and passed through the garden into the lane.

There was a magnificent view from the cottage across the Usk valley to the Black Mountains in the blue distance, extending in a line on the horizon. There was the pointed Sugar Loaf and Blorenge, others I have forgotten the names of and in between, the beautiful countryside of Monmouthshire. South of the Black Mountains and the Brecon Beacons the terrain changed dramatically into the mining valleys of South Wales.

Twice a year I used to go and stay at the cottage, once in the school Easter holidays and once in the summer. Auntie and Uncle drove up to the southern end of the Malvern Hills, to a place called Hollybush, where we met them, my parents having driven down from Birmingham.

Hollybush is adjacent to a wide area of open common land next to the Tewkesbury to Ledbury road. My mother told me there was an infantry camp during the First World War nearby on the common at Welland near Malvern for soldiers training before they went to fight in France. Considering that she had three brothers going to fight in France I think she must have visited at least one of them there.

When we met up with Auntie and Uncle and their family we'd have a picnic, the grown-ups would catch up on all the news and then I would get into their car and travel back to the cottage with them, waving goodbye to my parents as they set of to drive the thirty miles or so back to Birmingham.

Sometimes my parents took me all the way, after all it was only seventy miles but the roads were narrower than they are today and there were often underpowered lorries which would cause delays on the hills.

After getting to Monmouth there was a three mile

climb up a winding road to the cottage at Lydart. Pulling into the side of the road so my mother could powder her nose and make sure her hair was tidy was a necessity but I was impatient to get there. The nearer we got to the cottage the more excited I became.

Ahead was a week of freedom for me, freedom from the strictures of home, freedom to have fun with other children and to roam in the countryside. My parents were very strict and as an only child I felt it was all directed at me. They meant well and just wanted what was best for me but at times, particularly as I grew older, it became suffocating. My mother had strong views on diet but it would have been nice to be a bit more relaxed about it at times.

A week at the cottage was freedom indeed. I was allowed to have sugar on my cereal, white bread, even egg and bacon for breakfast. What treats!

Staying with a family of three children gave a lighter atmosphere to the days as well. We would play in the fields, cycle along the lanes and go on expeditions to the Black Mountains. Often in the summer evenings everyone would go for a walk around the local lanes where the sweet smell of honeysuckle lingered on the evening air and there was rarely any traffic. We were accompanied by the family corgi, Dilys, and often the cat would come along as well, stalking along behind us, her tail erect, pretending, as cats do, to have nothing to do with the people in front of her.

A favourite spot for expeditions was the Grwyne

Fawr valley. We'd all pile into Uncle's old Land Rover with a primus stove and baskets of delicious picnic food and off we'd go. The route lay through Abergavenny and on into the mountains with refreshing breezes bringing scents of heather, bracken and wet grass, smells that even now remind me of those days and the fun we had on those expeditions.

Sometimes en route we'd visit the tiny 11th century church at Partrishow. Auntie and Uncle were very keen on the architecture and history of these country churches. Partrishow, famous for its 16th century rood screen, is such a charming place and in a delightful setting on a sloping hillside. Next to the church is a small stable and in days gone by the visiting preacher put his horse in there during the service.

My husband and I were staying near Crickhowell on the Glannusk estate several years ago when we went to Partrishow one Sunday morning and attended the morning service. The congregation was very small and it was so peaceful, out of this world, almost literally, in its remote location.

After a visit to the church with Auntie and Uncle we were all keen to get on with the picnic. Uncle drove along the rough track by the river and a suitable place was chosen. We climbed excitedly out of the Land Rover and helped to unpack the food; out came a large freshly baked white loaf, eggs, bacon, butter and a huge tin of apricot jam. Auntie got the primus stove going and started to fry bacon in the frying pan that she had brought along. I wonder if she had two frying pans and two primus stoves, after all there were probably seven or eight of us on the trip because often their children brought friends along as well. Imagine the wonderful aroma of bacon cooking beside that mountain stream? What an idyllic setting it was.

After the bacon and egg had been eaten we bit hungrily into the thick slices of soft white bread that Auntie had spread with Welsh butter; tangy apricot jam was spooned onto them from the tin. Even the thought of it now makes me salivate.

When a suitable length of time had elapsed to allow our lunch to settle we put on bathing costumes and plunged into the icy stream. I'm not sure that we felt the cold. It was such fun splashing around in that deep pool, formed where a waterfall tumbled down from the bracken covered hillside to the place where the stream widened.

Somehow my parents never managed to organise such exciting outings. We sometimes took a friend of mine with us and went out into leafy Warwickshire or to British camp on the Malvern Hills in Worcestershire but although we took a picnic my mother never did the sort of delicious fry up that Auntie organised.

I concluded that my parents had had their fun before the war, before I came along. They went camping then, sometimes taking my mother's nephew Eric with them but after the war they were older and somehow the time had passed. And then increasingly as I moved into my teens my mother had osteoarthritis in her back and was often in a lot of pain. I always looked forward with eager anticipation to those holidays in that long white cottage on the edge of the Forest of Dean where Auntie Sylvia and Uncle Ken lived.

It's wonderful walking country around the Grwyne Fawr and climbing higher, along the track and beyond the reservoir, you find yourself looking down into the Wye valley and over towards Hay-on-Wye. It's Francis Kilvert country and you can read about places this country vicar wrote about in his Diaries when he was curate at Clyro in East Wales from 1865 to 1872. The ruins of Llanthony Priory and Capel-y-ffin, mentioned in his diaries, can be reached on foot by walking over the bracken covered hills into the next valley. They evoke past times when monks tilled the land and lived a life of prayerfulness.

It was on a peaceful Sunday afternoon that I gave Auntie Sylvia a terrible fright. A friend of one of the children had ridden his pony up to the cottage. I asked if I might 'have a go' on the pony and as there appeared to be no good reason why not I mounted the steed, stirrups were adjusted and I set off down the steep lane. All went well at first but the pony suddenly decided to head for home and started to career down the lane at a frightening speed.

Auntie and Uncle were enjoying a quiet cup of tea on the terrace in front of the cottage when suddenly they heard the clattering of hooves and the commotion of children shouting at the pony to stop. Auntie was horrified when she saw me racing past as the pony ran away down the hill. She stood up,

'Ken, get the car out!' she called in alarm.

Meanwhile I was getting quite frightened as I realised we were heading for the main road. It seemed wise to try to get off the pony; I managed to get my feet out of the stirrups. Seeing the nettles at the side of the road I made a jump for it.

My aim has never been very good and I landed on my back on the hard road. As I sat up Uncle arrived with the Land Rover. I think he was relieved to see that I was still alive. I was helped into the car and driven back to the cottage. Auntie was also relieved that the only injuries seemed to be a nasty graze where most of the back of my shirt had been left on the road. I was put in a warm bath, given an aspirin and a glass of warm milk and sent to bed to recover.

I don't remember being told off, I expect Auntie was glad not to be phoning my parents to say I was in hospital, but I expect strong words were issued to the other children about never again letting a visitor ride a strange horse.

On another occasion we all went to Raglan to do some gardening for a family friend. Her name was Horatia and I was terribly impressed when I was told she was the great, great granddaughter of Horatio Nelson by Lady Hamilton.

Other expeditions were made to some of the border castles and I particularly remember visiting White Castle which dates from the Middle Ages but by 1538 it and the nearby castles of Grosmont and

Skenfrith were abandoned. These expeditions were enjoyable days out but they were also history lessons when I began to learn about the Welsh Borders and the power struggles that had taken place in the area.

Through all these enjoyable excursions I was forming an interest in architecture, history and the landscape around me. A few years later when I was in the sixth form at Grammar School in Birmingham, studying A Level Geography, I went again to stay with my godparents. Uncle spent a day giving me a tour of South Wales showing me the contrast between the grim coal mining valley of Ebbw Vale not far from the beautiful valley of the River Usk and explaining to me the geology of the area.

Evenings at the cottage were peaceful and as I grew older I became aware that in their own sitting room, away from the children, classical music was being listened to on the radio. As an adult now I can appreciate what a joy that must have been with the scents of roses, lilies and honeysuckle in the garden drifting in through open windows in the summer and the incredible view from the sitting room windows over the fields, woodland and farmsteads towards the blue mountains in the distance.

I try now to analyse why the atmosphere in that home was so different from my own. In neither home, unlike my mother's sister's home, were there arguments, both marriages were loving and enduring.

I think Uncle Ken and Auntie Sylvia's backgrounds must have been different from that of my parents, more cultured. I think they had the advantage of a better education and homes where there were not the severe financial problems that my parents' families faced.

In contrast, my father left school at fourteen; despite undoubtedly having the ability to go to Grammar School his family just couldn't afford for him not to go out to work as soon as possible. Already when he left school his father had given up his job as a sporting gun action maker because he had gone blind and was slowly dying of cancer of the nose. His mother had to take in sewing to try to make ends meet. My mother's family were also in financial difficulties when she was a child because of an absent father, although by the time she left school money was a little easier.

In the twentieth century before 1945, children from working class and lower middle-class families had to leave school at the school leaving age which was thirteen or fourteen and go out to work. Their income was essential for many families and if you wanted to get ahead in the world or further your education you had to go to night school. And that is what my father did; he worked all day and then studied in the evening. He was very determined to reach his full potential by studying hard to become a draughtsman and an engineer.

After 1945, children who passed the 11 plus exam could go to Grammar School so the parents who could not afford school fees for the more prestigious schools were now able to see their children receiving an education that, in the words of the 1944 Education Act, was 'suitable for their age, aptitude and ability'. No longer was a child's education completely dependent on their parent's income. Although even then children from poorer families who were at Grammar School often had to leave at the then school leaving age of fifteen or sixteen and go out to work to supplement the family's income but at least they had spent five years receiving an education that suited their ability.

Connie and George, who had an adopted son Peter, were friends of my parents. I wasn't very keen on Peter who told what I then considered to be dirty stories, quite normal for a small boy though. I was also put off by the fact that I was made to wear his cast-off socks. He went to a private school called Stanley House School whose uniform was grey and royal blue so the socks in question were grey scratchy wool knee length socks with a couple of blue bands round the top. What an indignity being made to wear a boy's cast-off socks! Maybe this was another case of post war austerity, you didn't throw anything away if it could still be used.

As was the custom, they were Auntie Connie and Uncle George to me. Auntie Connie had been my mother's bridesmaid in 1927 so that friendship went back a long way. Auntie Connie was very clever at sewing and in my teenage years she gave me some sewing lessons because being left-handed didn't go down well in sewing classes at Grammar School. The plump and bespectacled teacher, Miss Evans, couldn't work out how to teach someone who did everything back to front so I found myself side-lined.

Surprisingly, at Westhill I had been made to write with my right hand but I always continued to draw and sew with my left hand. I remember at Grammar School my geography teacher being astounded that I was writing with my right hand while holding the crayon ready for colouring in maps with my left hand. Later when I was teaching I had no problem teaching right-handed children to sew as you just had the child facing you instead of standing by your side. Also, rather oddly, I wrote on the blackboard with my left hand, an asset because it means your body is not obscuring what you are writing.

Auntie Connie attempted to put right what I had missed at school. I felt she was a rather sad lady. I think she would have liked to have a daughter and I know she wanted to be close to me but somehow, I couldn't reciprocate the feeling.

Uncle George was a quiet man who worked at the Museum and Art Gallery off Chamberlain Square in Birmingham, a place I loved to visit as a child with my mother. A magnificent entrance led in from the street and a grand staircase rose to the upper floor. I remember the beautiful Pre-Raphaelite paintings and the intriguing collection of stuffed animals in glass cases in the Museum.

One day we found a Roman coin in our garden and took it in to Uncle George to be identified. I think the conclusion was that it was a gaming coin. He gave me a box of stamps taken from envelopes that had arrived there from the Museum's worldwide correspondence. I don't think stamp collecting was my forte though, probably a bit too fiddly for someone who is not a perfectionist.

At some stage, probably when I was in my mid-teens, Dad became a Mason and joined St Augustine's Lodge which met at Edgbaston. He played the organ for their meetings and they also had a choir. Through this he made some friends who, with their wives, used to meet from time to time at each other's houses for musical evenings at which the music of Gilbert and Sullivan was very popular.

When I was in my late teens I joined them too. Most of that group were in their sixties by then. Mrs Jordan, whose husband was a bank manager, was a brilliant pianist and could play anything by sight. Her husband, a portly gentleman with a very expressive face surmounted by dark hair brushed across his brow, possibly to disguise advancing baldness, would often give a wonderful rendition of 'I've got a Little List' from the Mikado. He had us all smiling with that.

Mr and Mrs Davies, a quieter couple who nevertheless made a good musical contribution were also part of the group. And there was Ted Vaughan Jones, a BBC singer, and his wife. Also, Uncle Stan Finchett, a jeweller, and his wife Auntie Nora, old friends of my parents. The Jordan's son Harry, who by that time was in his late twenties and a teacher of deaf children, was also part of the group. At what point people started linking his name with mine I do not know but certainly his mother was getting hopeful.

I met these people again when I went to the Masonic Ladies Nights once or twice when I was home from college. I had been to ballroom dancing classes with a friend; I must have learnt the basics of the quickstep and waltz but chiefly I remember the young lady teacher who clasped me firmly to her well-developed bosom and took the man's role. I enjoyed dancing with my father who did a very good quickstep.

I also danced with Harry and I think both Mrs Jordan and my mother may have hoped by that stage that romance was in the air. I know my parents thought marriage to a bank manager's son would be a good match and Mrs Jordan may have thought that as Harry and I were both teachers it would also be suitable. But it was not to be for at the next Ladies Night I was wearing my engagement ring. Mrs Jordan had missed the announcement in the Birmingham Post and she was visibly shocked.

The friends I have mentioned so far were relations or friends of my parents but I did make a friend entirely of my own and that was Judith. When I was nine I was sent to Miss Winifred Segust L.R.A.M. for piano lessons on Saturday mornings. I walked there from our house, crossing the Bristol Road and continuing along Cob Lane. Miss Segust lived in a small bungalow not far from there. It was very small and may have been specifically for disabled people as Miss Segust walked with the aid of leg irons. This could have been the result of having polio, for in her childhood children were not vaccinated against it as they were in my childhood.

This disability didn't prevent her from being a piano teacher and her small sitting room was dominated by a large black grand piano leaving room only for two arm chairs. When I arrived for my first lesson she already had a pupil seated at the piano who was just finishing her lesson. And that was how I met Judith.

Throughout the following years her lesson preceded mine on Saturday mornings and while Judith completed her lesson Miss Segust's black cat, Tiggy, used to install itself on my lap. In later years, we used to laugh about the efforts Miss Segust made to get us to play Handel's 'The Arrival of the Queen of Sheba' as a duet. I always played the lower part and Judith did the more complicated upper part.

Throughout the following years not only did we meet at our piano lessons but as our friendship developed we went to each other's houses, went out with each other's families and walked in the country together. Judith was just a few months younger than me and thus was in the school year below mine. Like me, she trained to be a teacher.

Coincidentally, she did her teacher training in Chichester which is where I live now when I am not in France and she was one of my bridesmaids at my wedding in 1964. However, I'm jumping ahead of my story so now it's time to go back to what happened after I left Westhill.

18. Susie and her parents with Eric, Joan and Nora

19. Joan on the left with Louise and Philip

20. Cousin Phil's wedding March 1951

21. On Bournemouth beach. Uncle Len, Auntie Glad,
Phil and Peggy.

22. On Guernsey for Susie's twelfth birthday

23. From the left: Mum, Uncle Ken, Dad and Auntie Sylvia

24. Uncle Percy

*25. Uncle Stan as Worshipful Master of St Augustine's Lodge
with Auntie Nora, greeting my parents on Ladies Night*

Chapter Five
School Days

My eleventh birthday was in August 1953 and the preceding January I had taken three eleven plus exams. The first was for the prestigious King Edward High School which I failed. Secondly on a cold January day I went to George Dixon Grammar School and took the exam for the Birmingham Grammar Schools which I passed. I also took the eleven plus exam for Bromsgrove Grammar School, just in case, and passed that.

It was decided that I would go to George Dixon's and I was pleased because my friend Roberta, from Westhill, hoped to be going there the following year. However, when she arrived at the school I had made other friends in my year, Roberta made friends in her year group and we didn't have much to do with each other from then on.

That summer, in 1953, before I started at Grammar School, we had a change from the usual and sometimes wet holiday at Llanbedrog and flew from Elmdon Airport, now Birmingham Airport, to Guernsey. My parents had known Elmdon before it was an airport when it was still called Elmdon Park. It had been a popular spot for their ten-year courtship.

It was the first time any of us had flown in an aeroplane. It was interesting coming in to land at

Guernsey; to see the island from the air with the bays and headlands laid out below like a map and where the glass houses for growing tomatoes were a notable feature of the landscape.

The weather was more reliable than in North Wales and we enjoyed swimming on the golden beaches, walking along the many little lanes on the island and exploring the capital of St Peter Port.

We went by boat to Sark where there were no cars and made the shorter trip across the water from St Peter Port to the tiny island of Herm where we were fascinated by the remarkable Shell Beach. My mother sat there on the warm sand letting the tiny pink shells trickle through her fingers. This was very different from Llanbedrog beach. My father only had two weeks holiday a year and wanted to spend this precious time swimming and lying on a warm beach rather than in wet Welsh drizzle.

The Channel Islands had been occupied by the Germans in the summer of 1940 and, although prior to that thirty thousand people had been evacuated, mainly from Alderney, the remaining sixty thousand people stayed on the islands. There was a curfew between 11pm and 5am, people had to carry identity cards and owning a radio became illegal. A register was kept of Jewish people and some were deported to concentration camps. There was no organised resistance as there was in France but there was an underground newsletter; people helped their Jewish neighbours and there were minor acts of sabotage.

Our holiday there was in the summer of 1953, only eight years since the end of the war. People told us of the indignity and inconvenience of having the hated German soldiers billeted on them. I was shocked when I saw one woman, with tears streaming down her face as she re-lived the morning she'd gone downstairs to find that the soldiers billeted on her had shot her much-loved dog and it was lying dead on the floor.

After the D-Day landings of 1944 the food supplies from the continent were cut off and everyone on the islands began to starve. After negotiations, the Germans allowed the Red Cross ship SS Vega to deliver food which saved the lives of many of the islanders. The Germans didn't leave the islands until 1945 despite being driven back from nearby Normandy and Brittany.

I had reached puberty that summer of 1953. Hormones had started to disrupt my life and the relationship with my parents had begun its slow decline. In other words, I had already started to mildly kick over the traces.

In September I donned my new school uniform, walked down to Selly Oak and, in Oak Tree Lane, caught the Number 11 Outer Circle bus which went via Harborne and the Hagley Road to City Road. The word 'lane' may give you the idea that Selly Oak was in the country but that was not the case. It was and is, a busy Birmingham suburb situated on the Bristol Road which goes south from the city through part of Edgbaston, Selly Park, Bournbrook, then Northfield,

Longbridge and finally on to Worcester. Travelling on the trams at first and later the buses, you could reach the Lickey Hills, a beautiful wooded area that was a popular destination for Birmingham people to walk, picnic and enjoy themselves.

By this time the influx of immigrants from the Caribbean had been going on for some time and we were used to seeing them as drivers and conductors on the buses and as nurses in the hospitals. Some of the men were returning after having served in the Forces during the war but they all came to seek a better life and to help rebuild Britain. They were missing the blue skies and warm sunshine of the Caribbean and were trying to become accustomed to the cold weather. Sometimes they faced hostility when signs like 'No Blacks Here' appeared in some boarding house windows.

Thus, I started my seven-year stint at George Dixon's. There was a two-form entry that year and which class you were in depended on where your name came in the alphabet. My surname being Williams, determined that I was in the second class with two other girls whose surname was also Williams so there was me, Andrea Williams and Joy Williams. And sitting behind me was Mary Willetts who lived at Halesowen and became a great friend. Nearby was Judith Wilson who also became a friend. I was probably the youngest in the class as my birthday is at the end of August.

The uniform was bottle green and red so we had bottle green gabardine raincoats, bottle green berets and bottle green gymslips. The gymslips must surely be one of the most unfashionable garments ever invented. As our female figures developed the pleats gradually spread further apart across our burgeoning bosoms. The whole lot was anchored by a green belt around our waists. We wore white shirts with red and green striped ties and bottle green cardigans. In the summer, we had a choice between green or red checked gingham dresses. Underneath that we wore bottle green knickers, elasticated at waist and leg. When we reached the Sixth form we wore skirts. For PE lessons we wore navy-blue knickers and white aertex shirts and for outdoor games we wore bottle green shorts, quite long of course, stopping just above the knee.

It was very strange at first being in a school where you had to move around to different classrooms when the bell rang to denote the end of the lesson. There were six classrooms around the school hall where the daily assembly was held. From the back of the hall a corridor led to the rooms used for sewing lessons and cookery classes and a staircase that led up to the science laboratories and the gym.

At the other end of the hall was a stage, to one side of which was the school library. Two sets of swing doors led out of the hall on each side of the stage; on one side a corridor led to the headmistress's office, the secretary's office, the medical room and the main entrance to the school which pupils were only allowed to use when they were in the sixth form.

Leaving the hall, in the other direction after

passing the lavatories and washroom, a covered way led to a line of classrooms and a quadrangle in which were two ugly huts used as classrooms. From the quadrangle, a long corridor led to the entrance used by most of the pupils, which was at the back of the primary school and near to the school canteen and the playing fields. Strategically placed away from the other classrooms on that long corridor was the music room.

This was the domain of the music teacher, Miss Mary Barber who was a delightful person with a neat wavy hairstyle and rimless glasses. She was a very accomplished musician. I enjoyed the lively piano music she played every day as we went into assembly and I belonged to the school choir and madrigal group which she taught. From time to time they performed in front of the school and parents at concerts and speech days. I will never forget the way Miss Barber smiled encouragingly at us when we were standing on the stage waiting to start singing. She would be in front of us, hands raised ready to conduct us, make sure we were all watching her, smile and then start. I never remember a cross word from her. She was always positive and encouraged us to do our best and of course we were only too keen to please her.

During the first year at George Dixon's the priority was to learn the school song based on the school motto, 'Strenue Agas', work hard.

'On the edge of the city,
Mid meadows green,

The towers of the school
To the north are seen.
Sturdy it stands
'Neath a wintry sky,
Unmoved by the winds
As they whistle by.
The home of the red and green.

'Strenue agas' be it dark or bright,
A friend to help or a wrong to right.
This motto shall live in the hearts of all,
Who worked or played in the old school hall,
The home of the red and green.

It was sung on many school occasions in the school hall, the home of the red and green.

My form mistress in the first year was Miss Saul, a kind, well-built lady who eventually realised that I had little aptitude for maths but who spent several years trying to instil some mathematical knowledge into me.

I was summoned to meet her outside the staff room door one day when she thrust the book containing my maths homework in front of me. However, the summons was not related to whether the sums were right or wrong but to the appearance of my work.

'Look at that,' she said. 'It's a mess'. And it was. Under each sum when it was finished I had ruled a line in ink and in each case the end of the line had slipped. 'You'll have to do better than that.'

My writing was awful too. It still is and I think it is something to do with being made to write with my right hand. Fortunately, when I was teaching I reverted to writing with my left hand, on the blackboard at least, and I'm glad to say it turned out to be neater than my right-handed attempts. Nowadays most of my writing is done on the computer so it's legible.

Many of our teachers were maiden ladies. They were from the generation whose potential husbands had been killed in the first world war. There was little Miss Montgomery 'Monty', who taught Latin; Miss Player hobbled around with arthritic feet and was reputed to have no toes, quite untrue I'm sure; her subject was History. Miss Whitefoot, an attractive English teacher, joked that her nickname was probably Blackhead, but I don't remember that it was.

Miss McCulloch also taught English. One day when a small group of us were in the Sixth Form she looked at us and said,

'How can you tell if a person is well educated?'

I apparently supplied the correct answer when I said,

'You can tell by the way people speak.'

On reflection that probably didn't mean whether they had a regional accent or not but that their grammar was correct. Occasionally I was called a snob as I did not have the local 'Brummie' accent but not everyone did.

I remember one speech day a town councillor came to distribute the prizes and give the obligatory speech. It was full of grammatical errors such as 'we was' and dropped aitches. I wonder if he felt inadequate as he stood there among the teachers in their academic gowns. At the time, I tended to look down on him for his appalling speech but with hindsight I think he was to be applauded for not letting his lack of education stop him serving his city as a councillor and for his bravery in standing up to give a speech among such highly educated ladies some of whom had Oxbridge degrees. This is an example of hindsight bringing a new perspective to events.

Miss Lodge, a very pleasant lady, taught cookery and among one of the first lessons was the one where we were taught to make sandwiches. We had to make sure that we buttered the bread right to the edge so that we didn't have dry unpalatable sandwiches and we had to cut the crusts off too. As that was before sliced bread was available I think we had to learn to slice bread very thinly. Learning to make leek and potato soup was another early lesson. It was delicious and is still one of my favourite soups to make.

I don't remember whether it was for cake making or pastry making that I took in wholemeal flour it being 'de rigeur' in my mother's healthy diet regime but I remember Miss Lodge trying to be encouraging and probably knowing full well that wholemeal flour for pastry wasn't as appetising or as successful as white flour.

However, my mother made some very delicious cakes with wholemeal flour and her little raisin cakes went down very well as did her chocolate cake with chocolate butter icing.

The gym was next to the biology lab and once a week we changed into our navy-blue knickers and white aertex shirts and swarmed up and down wall bars and vaulted over boxes. Miss Gray and Miss Britton were our teachers and they also took us out onto the sports field beyond the canteen to play hockey and netball in the winter and rounders and tennis in the summer. The 'wind whistling by' that is mentioned in the school song was very much in evidence during winter sports lessons outside as behind the school was a wide expanse of open land where the sports fields of three schools joined together. They were the playing fields for the two boys' grammar schools, George Dixon Boys and King Edward Five Ways Boys and ours.

The boys and girls Grammar Schools of George Dixon, although attached, were quite separate and we had nothing to do with the boys officially although I seem to remember we got quite excited when they passed beneath our classroom windows along a narrow pathway on the way to their games field. The boys' school was next door on City Road and beyond that there was St Germain's Church on the corner of Portland Road where occasionally the school held services.

At the end of our first year we had exams in all subjects including French. Those who did well commenced Latin lessons in the Autumn; the rest of us had German lessons. I had German lessons for three years. Regrettably my knowledge of the German language after those three years was negligible; the reasons will soon become apparent.

The first teacher was a young and severe woman called Miss Firth. She had been teaching at an army school in Germany before she came to us and her barking voice and abrupt ways may have been copied from the parade grounds there. Did she really call us cows or have I imagined that? Her manner of treating us did not endear her to us. Her idea of teaching us German was to write copious notes of the various declensions on the board for us to copy and learn parrot fashion. I for one, hadn't the remotest idea what declensions were. She taught us in one of the two huts, temporary classrooms in the school quad which were not included in the school's heating system but each had a temperamental cast iron stove at the back which was fed by coke and very smelly, probably producing carbon monoxide which could account for the low level of learning.

In the summer, it appeared that Miss Firth was getting married shortly after the end of term and a group of us thought that, as a bit of fun we would rig up a box of confetti to land on her head as she came through the door. I have a feeling the plan didn't quite work but I think it was the only time I saw her smile.

Another memory I have of Miss Firth is when she was doing dinner duty in the school canteen adjacent to the sports field. I found an ant in my pudding. There was the jam roly poly, there was the custard and there in the custard was the ant. I went up to her,

'Miss Firth, I've found an ant in my pudding.'

Her brusque reply was,

'Think yourself lucky you're not the ant!' I was filled with teenage outrage.

Now I think,

'What a fuss about nothing.'

The following term we were taught by a sad, dark haired, bespectacled middle-aged German lady with a strong accent. This must have been in 1955, exactly ten years after the war had ended.

At that time, I knew little about the war, even less about refugees and nothing at all about Jews who had fled from the Nazis. She must have been a refugee but whether she was Jewish or not I do not know but she was certainly sad and I fear that our progress with learning her native language can have done nothing to cheer her up.

The following year the disastrous story of our attempts to learn German continued when we had yet another teacher. She may have been called Mrs Scrivens and although I am uncertain of her name I am certain that we tried to make her life as difficult as possible.

The poor woman suffered badly from hay fever so to delay the start of the lesson we put any vases of flowers that were decorating the classroom on her desk to make her sneeze and to waste time at the start of the lesson.

'Good afternoon, atishoo, girls', she'd say. 'Lovely flowers but we'll have to, atishoo, move them. My hay fever's bad today'.

Her discipline was negligible and during what remained of the lesson several girls used to get changed for swimming, for which we departed as soon as the German lesson was finished.

'Are some girls missing today?' she'd ask not realising that they were sitting on the floor under their desks struggling to put their swimming costumes on.

Mostly we didn't play the teachers up but Miss Curry, who taught Religious Education, also proved ripe for some time-wasting behaviour. This Scottish lady with her frizzy hair, dressed in sensible bluey-green tweeds was very fond of fresh air. Before the lesson we made sure all the windows were closed.

'Och girrls,' she'd say, 'it's awfu stuffy in here. We must open some windows'.

And then there would be a hunt for the window pole, carefully hidden beforehand, of course. So that was some time wasted. I was careful not to get involved in baiting Miss Curry for she came to our church and I didn't want her telling my parents how naughty I was.

The incident of the ant in my pudding reminds me of a cruel joke I played on a girl called Margaret Siviter who was in my class. That also occurred in the school canteen. There was one pudding that was a favourite of ours. It was a type of lemon meringue. Aluminium trays were used for many of the foods and the ones used for puddings were shallower than the ones used for example, for the gristly shepherd's pie. The shallow trays were lined with a particularly soggy pastry which then had a sickly yellow lemon flavoured substance poured into them. After they were cooked and cooled they were cut into portions and each one had a small piece of meringue place on it. Many of us saved our precious bits of meringue at the side of our plates to savour when we'd finished our pudding. Poor Margaret had done that and when her attention was elsewhere I stole her meringue and ate it. She was justifiably outraged.

On another occasion when we'd had a cookery lesson I found her in the washroom licking a mixture of left over cocoa and sugar off a piece of greaseproof paper. I flicked the paper and the cocoa went all over her face and down her throat and made her cough violently. Poor Margaret; how unkind I was to her. She was actually a very pleasant girl. If you ever read this, Margaret, please accept my heartfelt apologies for being so unkind to you.

A delightful lady called Mrs Sweet taught us art which was not only painting and drawing but the history of art as well. I enjoyed hearing about Fra Angelico and his frescoes.

Miss Whelan, who taught French, married in our second year at school and became Mrs Fox. She took us on a remarkable school trip which I believe must have been most unusual at the time. Miss Gray, Miss Mason and a teacher from another school, Miss Falla accompanied our group.

Mrs Fox was a leader in the Girl Guide movement and was friendly with a teacher from a girls' school in Evreux, a town in northern France. The main purpose of the trip was to spend three weeks in a bi-lingual camp at Vallouise in the Dauphiné Alps in France with the girls from Evreux. We travelled from New Street Station in Birmingham to London and thence to Folkstone on the boat train. There were fourteen of us. The names of some of the other girls who went on the trip were Pearl Jones, Gina Knight, Judith Wilson, Suzanne Gooden, Gillian Richards, Judith Stone, Andrea Williams, Monica Elton, Judith Poynter and Valerie Spencer. There were also three other girls whose names I cannot remember.

The boat to Calais from Folkestone was very much smaller than the ferries of today. Travelling on the boat was a group of French singers from Brittany who had been to the Eisteddfod at Llangollen. They sang and danced for the passengers and not only was it delightful but it helped the journey to pass.

When we disembarked at Calais we crossed the platform to the train waiting to take us to Paris.

How exciting! We were in France at last and looking out of the window we wondered what we could see that would show we were in a different country. We didn't have long to wait for as we passed through the agricultural area of northern France we were amazed to see a man walking behind a single plough pulled by a horse. He was laboriously struggling to keep a straight furrow. It reminded me of a picture of agriculture in the Middle Ages.

Eventually the train pulled into Gare du Nord, the terminus in Paris. Different sights, smells and language were all around us and so were crowds of people jostling us. A friend of Mrs Fox came to collect us with a mini-bus and took us off to St Michel in the Latin Quarter where we were to stay at a Lycée.

I have a dim recollection of entering a large austere stone building where we went up four flights of wide wooden stairs to a dormitory where we each had a small wooden cubicle. This being mid-July term had ended and the students who were usually in occupation had gone back to their own homes and were scattered across France on holiday

For breakfast the following morning we had bread rolls and delicious coffee which we ate in the refectory. Mrs Fox and Miss Gray went out to shop for our picnic lunch and when they came back the food was shared out and we went off to start our day in Paris. Notre Dame was the first place on our sightseeing tour but our plan to go inside was thwarted as the funeral of an important policeman who had been killed on duty was being held there. While we were watching, mourners emerged from two cars which had just drawn up; the ladies deeply veiled in black. Sombre black-suited undertakers took colourful wreaths from the cortege and carried them inside the building. The square in front of the church was lined with policemen who looked very smart until we looked at their shabby unpolished shoes.

After visiting the Flower Market, we went to see the church of La Sainte Chapelle situated on the Ile de la Cité. I think it is one of the most beautiful churches I have ever seen with its soaring Gothic columns, beautiful stained-glass windows and painted ceiling.

La Sainte Chapelle was built sometime after 1238 to house Louis the Ninth's collection of the relics of Christ which included the Crown of Thorns. He purchased them from Baldwin the Second, Latin Emperor at Constantinople but the money was paid to the Venetians to whom the relics had been pawned. It seems even emperors can be hard up.

We walked along the side of the Seine under the plane trees where the second-hand bookstalls were and made our way to the Eiffel Tower. How can you go to Paris and not visit that?

We had walked a long way by then and it was lunch time so we rested under the trees and ate our food. A few of the girls went up the Tower but I bought some postcards and stayed with Mrs Fox and a few other girls. Rain and thunder prompted us to make for the Metro and then back to the Lycée.

After dinner, we went for a walk and visited the Luxembourg Gardens before settling down for our second night in Paris. Next day we were departing and had to pack after breakfast and write our diaries, which we did each day that we were away. Mrs Fox and Miss Gray went out again for food. We had the rest of the day for more sightseeing as our train to the south didn't depart until the evening. We walked across Paris to

Montmartre where the white marble church of Sacré Coeur was prominent on top of the hill. I remember going from the bright sunshine outside to the dark interior where seemingly a thousand candles twinkled in the gloom and incense was heavy on the air. Then by Metro to the Arc de Triomphe and a walk down the Champs Elysée.

I have a blurry photo which shows us at lunch time that day eating our picnic in front of the Louvre. Afterwards we went inside and saw the Mona Lisa and the Venus de Milo. Then it was back to the Lycée to have a rest and collect our luggage. I take my hat off to Mrs Fox and Miss Gray who had planned such an interesting introduction to Paris for us and were prepared to take the responsibility for that group of teenagers abroad. They must have been exhausted but they were only in their early twenties, not much more than ten years older than we were.

We caught the night train which went from the Gare d'Austerlitz to Gap and then up the Durance valley towards Briançon. On that hot evening the station was crowded not only with civilian passengers but with hundreds of soldiers. The French war with Algeria was becoming more intense and by now many young men had been conscripted to serve in the army. My world suddenly expanded as I saw raw human emotions as these brave young men were saying farewell to their mothers, fathers, wives and sweethearts. This wasn't playing at soldiers; this was for real.

I didn't know until sometime later that this scene must have been painful for Mrs Fox because at the time her husband was a serving soldier in Cyprus where periodically terrorist attacks took the lives of British servicemen.

Two compartments had been reserved on the train for our group and as we travelled south we tried to sleep while we were sitting up. From time to time we put our feet up on the lap of the person opposite but no-one had a good night's sleep so when we arrived the following morning at the station of L'Argentière we were very tired.

We were met by two of the French girls and had coffee in the town before catching the bus up to the village of Vallouise. Our luggage was sent along later.

Today the road up to the village, and the ski resort which has been built since those days, is wide and surfaced with tarmac but then it was not much more than a dusty cart track and the bus was a ramshackle affair that carried the local population up from the market in L'Argentière. Crates of hens and sacks of poultry food competed with passengers and their shopping for the available space.

No doubt this group of English girls and their teachers attracted some questioning glances and comments. It was not every day that the world came to this little backwater, unlike today when it is a popular holiday destination.

The French girls and their teachers had arrived a few days before us and when the bus stopped in the village near the bridge over the river they were there to meet us and walk with us up to the camp.

One of their teachers, given the nickname of Cèdre, walked alongside me and tried to engage me in conversation, not very successfully I'm afraid. It was all so strange, it was so hot, I was tired after the overnight journey and my French was appalling.

We crossed the river, walked through the village square by the church and along a small track that meandered out of the village passing a small shrine en route. After half a mile or so we crossed over another river on a plank bridge. The track started to climb through the trees. We were grateful for the shade as we were unaccustomed to the intense heat.

After another half mile, the track went around a large rock that jutted out over the path and then we saw in front of us a mountain torrent cascading down among rocks through the trees and on the opposite bank and up a slope, lay the chalet which was to be our headquarters. This was where we had our meals sitting outside on a terrace.

Underneath the building was the cave, the cellar, where traditionally animals would live in the winter but for the duration of our stay was where we kept our clothes. There was hay on the floor in which, during our stay there, I lost the brace I was wearing on my teeth at the time. Fortunately, after a frantic search I found it again; it was not quite as bad as losing a needle in a hay stack but it was a close thing.

In a meadow on the other side of the chalet three

large army tents had been set up; each one slept about ten girls on camp beds.

I had never been camping, I suppose few of us had, so we needed to get used to the washing and sanitary facilities. Our bathroom was the mountain torrent where we washed and cleaned our teeth in icy water; our toilets, behind canvas screens, were pits with a couple of boards across them.

This was by no means a luxury holiday, despite being in beautiful surroundings and, in true Guide fashion, the chores were shared out on a rota basis and we all had to muck in. Although a woman from the village came along to cook our meals we were expected to serve them and do the washing up.

That was the first time I ate the Petit Suisse cheese which was served with sugar or jam. Delicious. The spicy loaf, pain d'épices, was another food that was new to me and I enjoy buying that in France today.

The least popular of the chores was digging the latrines and covering up the used sections with earth.

Day to day activities on the camp were well organised with a short service of a bible reading and prayers each morning and the raising and lowering of the national flags, 'the Colours', each morning and evening. We also were taught how to tie knots and we learnt national dances and songs and thus shared our diverse cultures.

There was a project to produce a small magazine. I still have my copy after all these years. On the front is a lino cut with a mountain scene and pine trees.

Inside, Marie-Louise Viennois has written an article in French about these girls from different countries getting to know each other and learn each other's language. There is an article about the Guide International flag in English, an article in French about the Union Jack, one about the French Flag and the Revolution; two articles, one English, one French about the thought for the day and living together in friendship and how a violent mountain storm can change a peaceful scene into one of chaos just as a display of bad temper can spoil a whole day in camp. And lastly a ghost story written by my class mate, Andrea Williams, about the local priest. The magazine was quite an ambitious undertaking and there was a certain amount of pressure in the last few days to get it finished and printed.

We were encouraged to write in our diaries every day. I still have mine which has been useful for checking the details of that trip of sixty years ago.

After lunch we often had a siesta during which we could write home; any letters we wrote probably took nearly a week to get there. Apparently my first letter must have gone astray because I had a very curt note from my father which just said, 'Write home'. Perhaps feeling slightly homesick I had been looking forward to having a letter from home and was very hurt by his note. He was not known for his tact.

Apart from activities around the camp we went on some very interesting outings. One was to Briançon where we explored the interesting old walled town and

Vauban's fortifications. Briançon is situated near the border between Italy and France.

From there we went by coach to a cable car station, and rode the 'Teleferic' to the top of the ridge. We climbed up higher on a track and then over the top into the Eychauda valley. I have been there many times since that first visit and to some people that high treeless valley can seem very barren and austere but I love the space and the views of distant wooded valleys and mountain peaks, the highest among them in excess of eleven or twelve thousand feet, snow covered throughout the year.

The diary tells me we had tea at a smelly farmhouse on the way back to camp. Possibly goats were kept there which would account for the smell.

Another expedition was to the refuge above Glacier Blanc where we spent the night in bunk beds in a dormitory shared by men and women. I doubt if any of the serious climbers there were enamoured of the idea of spending the night with a school party of teenage girls.

It was exciting to climb from the Chalet Refuge at Prés de Madame Carle up a narrow, rocky path and across the glacier. Ropes had been fixed to the rocks to help climbers. The view from the refuge was astounding as we looked out at the peaks of Pelvoux and the Ecrins.

Today the route we took across the glacier is no longer there because the glacier has retreated considerably during the last sixty years and a newer refuge has replaced the one we slept in.

At that time, before tourism had swept into the valley, only serious climbers went that way. At the foot of the path up to the glacier is Prés de Madame Carle where today there is a huge car park and a camp site from which people swarm up the narrow track like ants.

A less demanding activity was going to pick lavender in the fields on the edge of the village. Here we were taught how to tie the stalks of the lavender with ribbon and then bend them back and weave the ribbon between the stalks to hold the lavender heads. I have made these delightful sweet smelling little baskets many times since then and they recall a lovely afternoon in the lavender fields of Vallouise.

One afternoon we went down to a fete in the village. Everything was very jolly and there was much stuffing of confetti down our dresses and into our mouths.

Eventually our time of camp life and learning to live together with girls of a different nationality came to an end and the flags were taken down for the final time. We made our last walk along the track and past the little shrine to the village. Little could I imagine then that I would revisit the village many times and even write a fictional book that is set there.

The French girls came up to Paris with us on the train and then went on to their homes in Evreux. We spent another night in Paris and then on 10th of August caught the train to Calais, the boat to Folkstone and finally from London, the train to Birmingham. Our French adventure and, for me, a time away from the constraints of home, had ended.

I have been back to Vallouise many times for holidays, both caravanning at the excellent site at Les Vigneaux with my family and to stay in a small hotel at Les Prés where in the meadows nearby in 1956 we had done national dancing in the fields.

***

I didn't find my time at Grammar School very happy. After I had been there for about two years my mother became increasingly unwell with osteoarthritis and both my parents thought I was becoming very difficult. Looking back on those days from their point of view I suppose I was. I was no longer the compliant child I had been. Like most teenagers I was beginning to flex the muscles of independence.

Mary Willetts, the girl I had become particularly friendly with, moved away with her family to live in Oxford. Mary and I used to visit each other's homes when she lived in Halesowen. Mary, and her mother, must soon have realised that my home was by no means as free and easy as hers was. She had two younger siblings James and Jane and with them used to wander the nearby fields and get quite messy. I remember Mary's mother being so concerned on one visit to her home about how filthy my white socks had become that she washed them and ironed them dry so I wouldn't get told off when I got home.

They were a lovely friendly family and I missed Mary very much when she moved away. I went to stay with her in Oxford later but sadly we lost touch after we both left school. I would love to know what happened to her. Maybe like me she became a teacher, I don't know, but I'm sure she must have married, had a large family and been a wonderful mother.

By the time Mary had gone, the other girls had friendships that were firmly established and I felt rather out on a limb. Having chosen to go out of my home area to Grammar School I had no local friends who went to the school. Other girls travelled on the bus with friends from their neighbourhood but I went home alone. Occasionally I used to visit some of them but I wasn't really part of their group and nothing lasted.

So, at school I had no very close friends with whom to discuss the way I felt towards my parents and as an only child I felt isolated. My parents were older than most parents and without a doubt they were somewhat set in their ways. My mother's family were very forthright about expressing their opinions and although she was less so, she did have the family trait to a certain extent.

And then there were her ideas on diet which today are quite normal but in those days taking wholemeal flour to school for cookery lessons and having salad and brown bread when anyone came home to tea was very unusual and added to my feeling of being 'different'. I don't think being adopted ever made me feel different though, probably because I knew several other children were in the same position.

My father had been born the year before Queen Victoria died and although I wouldn't go so far as to say he was Victorian in attitude he could be very single minded. To be fair he'd had to be; he wouldn't have got on as well as he did in life if he hadn't been determined to improve himself and catch up at night school with the education he'd missed with leaving school at fourteen.

Undoubtedly both my parents wanted the best for me and wanted me to make the best of my opportunities. But I sometimes found this oppressive. It sapped my confidence.

There was a girl at King Edward High School with the same name as mine. My parents knew of her because she was a friend of the daughter of another family they knew, who also went to the High School. We had also seen her perform in school plays there. She was a brilliant extrovert and eventually went on to Oxford.

On several occasions my father said to me,

'Why can't you be like the other Susie Williams?'

I felt suffocated by the unceasing negative comments about my behaviour, progress at school and whatever else they thought I should be doing. The judgemental comments at meal times coming from both of them used to send me shrieking from the table in a rage which caused my mother to collapse in tears and my father to chase after me trying to hit me. I'm not sure that he ever succeeded. Probably my mother's tears stopped him. I don't think this helped her health issues.

She used to encourage me to do my best and never compared me to the girl at the High School. But I know she discussed my behaviour with the next-door neighbour and I think they both decided they had never come across anyone who behaved as strangely as I did. None of this helped my confidence or improved the relationship with my parents.

It wasn't until I was at college and with other students discussed our home lives that I began to realise that I wasn't the only one who had had difficulties with their parents. I wasn't the only one who had to wear sensible shoes, be in at a certain time or felt their parents were odd. And it wasn't until many years later when we had problems with our teenage foster daughters that I realised that actually, my parents' knowledge of teenage girls had been very limited indeed.

Out of school Judith and I met up quite a lot. We only lived about half a mile apart. We used to go walking together and visit each other's homes. Her parents had relations living close by and Judith had her brother and a cousin of a similar age to herself. Again, it was all much more free and easy than in my own home.

My mother's elder brother, Cyril, was by now living next door because he had married Elsie, the widow who was living there when we moved in.

A few years before that it was Elsie's fifteen-year-old son who decided bizarrely one day he would catch me and take me to the end of the garden, take my knickers down and spank my bottom. At the time of the incident I was probably about nine. Did I tell anyone? No.

Today a court case would probably have been made from it and the boy would have been labelled a paedophile and been locked away. In fact it was just a stupid teenage prank.

Cyril had become no less domineering with age and that was additional stress for my mother, especially as he was now living next door.

One day she had arranged that we should meet him at 11am in Barrows. It was a shop that sold provisions, an old-fashioned word for food. And it was a somewhat old-fashioned shop. The entrance was in Corporation Street and led to the first part of the shop and then into a splendid Food Hall where large hams could be sliced for you. Upstairs there was a restaurant and a Ladies Rest Room; as well as the loos and basins that you would expect today, there was also a sitting room where you could rest on the easy chairs and meet your female friends in a refined atmosphere away from the hustle and bustle in the street.

We turned up at Barrows at the appointed time and place to meet Uncle and waited for him to arrive.

My mother kept looking at her watch.

'It's strange that he's not here,' she said. 'He's usually a stickler for punctuality.'

After we'd waited for about twenty minutes we suddenly saw him stride past us, walking far too fast for us to catch up with him. Later we discovered he'd been waiting just around the corner from where we were standing. And of course, being sure he was right, it never occurred to him that we would be waiting anywhere else so he didn't look around him as he stalked out of the shop. My poor mother got a forceful telling off from her big brother.

Nevertheless, he was a kindly man at heart and when he took a school party to Paris he returned with a bracelet for me with scenes of Paris on it and a model of the Eiffel Tower.

One day he took me to London for the day accompanied by my mother. We went on the train from Birmingham New Street. That was still in the days of steam trains when on entering a tunnel steam and smoke would billow around the train and windows had to be kept shut so you wouldn't end up with black smuts on your face. Part of the way along the journey a large tube descended from the train to scoop up water from the troughs at the side of the track as the train continued on its way; water was needed to make the steam to propel the train.

In London, we went to Madame Tussauds, had lunch at a Lyons Corner House and went to see Buckingham Palace.

He also gave me swimming lessons when my mother took me to him at the end of his day's teaching at King Edward Five Ways Grammar School.

Another old-fashioned shop in Birmingham was a haberdashers near the lower end of Corporation Street. Bolts of cloth lined the shelves and little drawers held buttons, cards of hooks and eyes and dozens of objects that were needed in sewing. Assistants stood at the polished wooden counters ready to serve the customers. When the purchase had been neatly wrapped in brown paper and tied up with string the bill was presented to the customer who produced the money. Then it and the bill were put in a container and inserted into a metal tube above the counter. As if by magic it would be sucked away to the accounts department with a whooshing noise. A few moments later another whooshing noise would announce its arrival back at the counter; madam would be given her receipt and any change that was due and thus the purchase was completed.

Shopping completed, the journey back to the bus in Navigation Street would begin, passing the offices of the Birmingham Post and Mail near the corner of New Street where a man selling hot baked potatoes always stood in the winter. He had an intriguing black metal cart that had an oven on it from which a tantalising smell arose. Underneath the oven was a drawer of hot coals to provide the heat and cook the potatoes. I don't remember that we ever bought any of his hot potatoes though the smell was wonderful on a cold day and I expect lots of people did.

Our route took us down into Stephenson's Place, in front of New Street Station towards Navigation

Street where we had a choice between the 61, 62 or 63 buses that would take us along the Bristol Road towards home.

The Alexandra Theatre was not far from Navigation Street and I went there with my parents to see Ivor Novello's 'The Dancing Years'. I loved the music, the dancing and the bright lights and the feeling of going out to something exciting in a dark evening. I have a vague memory of seeing Frankie Howard there too.

The old Birmingham Repertory Theatre was nearby and I went there several times but the visit I remember most clearly was in 1958, the year we studied Julius Caesar for 'O' Level English. Looking back, it seemed to me to be quite a small theatre with the seats rising very steeply from the stage. The main feature of that afternoon was wondering whether or not Caesar would fall off the stage as he rolled around in agony after he had been stabbed. I don't think he did but the actor did a good line in suspense.

I had been attending Carrs Lane Congregational Church with my parents since I was about ten. Before then I had been sent to the Sunday School at our local Parish Church, St Mary's, in Selly Oak, for a short time. They issued coloured stickers of the weekly Bible story when you attended and I had about a dozen of these which strangely I stuck to the inside of a drawer in the dining room at home.

I think my parents must have been thinking for some time that it was time we went to church as a family. We went a few times to the Quaker Meetings at Bournville and Kings Norton. I can't imagine that sitting in silence for an hour would have suited my father very well.

Carrs Lane Congregational Church was the church we eventually attended. Dad must have enjoyed the music played by the brilliant organist Dr Christopher. I went there until I was married. I joined the church when I was twenty-one and became a committed Christian, although it must be said, my beliefs are rather unorthodox.

Carrs Lane was, and is today in its new building, a church that provides many activities for its congregation. There were two services on Sundays and a Sunday School or Family Church, to which children in the congregation went out part way through the morning service. There was also a weekday club for adults called The Seventy Club, taking its name from the seventy apostles Christ sent out to spread the gospel.

There was also the Junior Seventy Club for young people. My parents tried to push me into joining that but the harder they pushed the more I resisted. However, I did join in with some week-ends the young people spent at Barnes Close, a Christian conference centre near Bromsgrove. Today it is run by the Community for Reconciliation, an ecumenical organisation.

The week-ends there were during the time Rev. Leslie Tizard was the minister at Carrs Lane. He was very highly thought of, as was his wife and they made a good team. But I felt very embarrassed once when he asked me to say grace before the meal.

'I wouldn't know what to say,' I mumbled in reply.

We never said grace at home and the closest I had been to anyone doing so was when we had a meal with Uncle Walter and Auntie Flo who, as Quakers, didn't say grace out loud but quietly bowed their heads and gave thanks in their own way. I have always thought that is very appropriate.

However, the week-ends at Barnes Close, with a mixture of talks, games and companionship were part of my Christian education. But I still could not be persuaded to join the Junior Seventy Club. In a way, it was like not being part of the circle of friends at school because it was not a local school. Neither was Carrs Lane Church, over five miles away, a local church. It was a bus ride away followed by a walk along city streets. The young people who attended it lived in other parts of Birmingham. Was I just lazy or shy? I was certainly lacking in confidence.

When I was fifteen I went to the Law Courts in Corporation Street when I was called as a witness to a fatal motor bike crash. I'd seen the collision between the bike and the car from the back seat of my parent's car. The youth had speeded past us and collided with a car some distance in front of us as it was turning right. I saw him fly into the air and a few moments later he was dead. What a tragic loss of life. I was too young to be in court for the whole of the case so was called in at the appropriate time.

The whole proceeding seemed to hinge on whether the car driver had signalled that he was turning right.

'Did you see the driver signalling?' I was asked.

'I couldn't be sure at that distance whether he was or not,' I replied.

Oh dear, the effort of calling me as a witness probably hadn't been worth it but it was an interesting experience for me and got me a mention in the paper.

I've often thought since then that these young men who enjoy speeding dangerously around in their cars and motor bikes on our roads today are the same age as the brave young men who went to the skies in the Battle of Britain in 1940. How grateful the nation was then for their love of speed and courage.

Around that time I began to get interested in boys in a minor way. At first there was Andrew who with his family came to our church. The two families were friends. He was a gentle, academic boy who went to the High School. We both liked classical music and occasionally went to concerts at the Town Hall together. Music by Grieg, Elgar, Dvorak, Gershwin and Copeland performed by the City of Birmingham Symphony Orchestra became favourites of mine.

Every year the Birmingham Grammar Schools had a Music Festival at the Town Hall to which each of the Grammar Schools contributed ten pupils to the choir. Both years that I was in the Sixth Form at school I was part of that choir. It was a tremendously uplifting experience as we sang with the City of Birmingham Symphony Orchestra. One year we sang Hayden's Third Mass. It was the only time I sang as part of a large choir and I enjoyed it very much.

There was another boy with whom I had a fairly intense friendship for a couple of years. We thought our friendship was IT but one day I suddenly decided that the opposite was true. And that was the end of that. He was terribly upset and couldn't understand why I had so suddenly changed my mind. Neither could I understand really but changed it I had and that was that.

My mother asked me,

'Had he done anything inappropriate?'

Knowing full well what she meant I replied,

'No, he hadn't. I'd just gone off him'. Actually, I'd got fed up with him showing off at the local swimming pool.

In 1958 I obtained a satisfactory number of 'O' Levels and the following Autumn went into the sixth form where I chose to study Geography and Biology for A Level.

Miss Gosling was my biology teacher and I enjoyed her lessons very much. Studying sections of plants under the microscope was fascinating and dissecting rats, although messy, was interesting too. One of the girls, when dissecting her rat's bladder, had the unfortunate experience of it squirting the contents in her face.

One day our homework was to write an essay on

manure. Apparently, I did quite a passable essay but missed Miss Gosling's joke when she announced to the class that I 'had covered the ground well'. Someone else pointed it out to me after the class.

Only four of us studied A level geography and although I enjoyed studying different aspects of the subject in more depth, the teaching, when pages and pages of notes were dictated to us, was a bit tedious. When Miss Ore said something was 'in situe' I hadn't a clue what she was talking about and in my notes, wrote down C2 because that was what it sounded like.

Her desk was on a raised platform and she was totally unaware that the desk had no front panel on it and so we had a good, if unwanted, view of her splayed legs and elasticated pink knickers.

The second year started with a week spent at Juniper Hall Field Studies Centre near Dorking and tramping around the countryside studying rivers and landscape provided the practical work that I had been enjoying in Biology.

It was the first trip away from the restrictions of home and parents for several of the students. Some of the boys who had come from a school in the south of England obtained some cider and one of them over imbibed, becoming quite drunk. Next day, amid pleas for leniency, he was sent home in disgrace. No one else was going to risk the same fate and everyone behaved themselves after that. The law was laid down as to what was acceptable behaviour and what was not.

Parameters were also discussed back at school

when the Scripture Group met in the sombre atmosphere of the school library and Canon Bryan Green, Rector of Birmingham and a great and famous evangelist, came to talk to us. Sombre may have been the surroundings but the atmosphere in the room was electric whenever he spoke.

He was outspoken in his recipe for the correct way to conduct ourselves with boys. There was a twelve-point scale of the way to proceed from holding hands and a gentle cuddle to a full and complete sexual relationship after marriage. Definitely only after marriage it must be noted. And generally, at that time that was what happened but obviously not always.

I think the idea was that you 'saved yourself' for when you were married and didn't lose beforehand what you could never regain. But, again with hindsight, that was all pre-pill and even the Family Planning Clinic would only see you if you were engaged and had a date for the wedding. How times have changed.

My father let me know in no uncertain terms that if I became pregnant before marriage I would be out. Yes, this was the time when girls who were 'caught out' went away to have their babies discreetly and were coerced into having them adopted. Fear of pregnancy was a big deterrent and being a single mother at a very young age would be very difficult.

In the last Spring half-term of my school days we had a week's holiday. I wonder if Dad's holiday allowance had gone up from two weeks to three because with my parents I went to stay at a guest house in Grasmere in the Lake District. All around me were the U-shaped valleys and roches moutonées, features of glaciation that I had been learning about in geography.

The date for my A level geography exam was drawing very close. The landlady of the guest house had kindly provided a small table in my room so that I could use it as a desk as I had to spend quite a lot of that holiday revising. Tearing myself away from the wonderful mountain views surrounding me I had to study the geography of South America.

When the exams were over I left school.

For the last two or three years my parents had decided that they would have a much more enjoyable holiday without their temperamental teenage daughter. I went to stay with either Uncle Percy and Auntie Madge at Tanworth-in-Arden or with Auntie Louise and Uncle Doug at Shirley or with some family friends who lived in Solihull. All these locations involved a lengthy trip into school either on the train from Wood End near Tanworth or by bus into town and then out the other side to Edgbaston on another bus. It made a change for me and I can't really blame my parents for wanting a more peaceful holiday.

I think it must have been the year before I left school my mother and I had a week's holiday in North Wales in August on our own. We went by coach from Birmingham to the Butlins Holiday Camp at Pwllheli and then on by taxi to a Country Club near Llanbedrog, the location of many childhood holidays.

I don't remember much of that holiday other than the rain. North Wales was true to type and without a car there wasn't a lot to do except walk along lanes dripping with water. Long days on the beach and swimming in the sea didn't feature in that holiday so I don't think it was very successful. Although I no longer went on the family holiday I did have that wet week in North Wales and I also continued my holidays with my godparents on the edge of the Forest of Dean which I look back on with great pleasure.

26. The Madrigal Group with Miss Barber at George Dixon's

27. Miss E. Gray and the School Party at New Street Station July 1956

28. Bi-lingual camp at Vallouise 1956

29. The chalet

30. The old refuge at Glacier Blanc at 2550 metres

31. Susie in the Alps

Chapter Six
Moving On

During my last year at school a decision had to be made about what I was going to do next. Getting into university was a lot harder at that time so it didn't seem to be an option for me as I was not highly academic. Physiotherapy was of some interest but probably thanks to Auntie Louise, I decide to apply to a teacher training college.

I had been into the infant school Auntie taught at several times and it seemed to be the way forward for me. But it was Juniors I wanted to teach.

I applied to Redland College in Bristol and my parents dutifully took me there for an interview. Having read about what an interesting city Bristol is I know I would have enjoyed my time there but it was not to be as I was not offered a place at the college. Fate had something else in store for me and the 'something else' turned out to be very satisfactory.

I went to an interview on 14th February 1960 at Kesteven Training College near Grantham, on my own, by train. When I look back on it, Valentine's Day was quite propitious as it turned out.

The plan was to go by train from Birmingham to Nottingham where, the timetable informed me, the fifteen minutes between the arrival of my train and the departure of the one for Grantham would be quite adequate to change between platforms.

Unfortunately, when I arrived in Nottingham I discovered that it wasn't a matter of changing platforms but of changing stations. The train from Birmingham arrived at Nottingham Midland Station and the one for Grantham departed from Nottingham High Level Station and there was insufficient time for me to walk between the stations and catch the train to Grantham.

Here was a dilemma; I was obviously not going to be at the interview in time. Oh dear, a black mark to start with. I found a phone box, telephoned the college and explained the situation, then walked to the correct station. This left me with some time in hand so I found a nearby café, had an egg on toast for lunch and eventually managed to get the train to Grantham. Then followed a five miles bus journey south along the Great North Road and a long walk up the college drive. This gave me time to appreciate the beautiful parkland in which the college was situated.

I was reminded that it was Valentine's Day when, half way up the drive, I was picked up by a florist's van and taken the rest of the way to the college.

The only thing I remember about the interview was when Mr Warmington, the College Principal, asked me to show him my hands. Was he looking to see if I was of such a nervous disposition that I bit my nails? Fortunately, I had given that bad habit up many years earlier.

He was not the cheeriest of people to be

interviewed by but I passed muster and a few days later received a letter informing me that I had been given a place to start a three-year teacher training course the following October. Now I knew what I would be doing for the next three years, or not, as it turned out.

I should point out here that this was the year that teacher training was changing from a two-year course to a three-year course. To overcome the lack of any teachers emerging from training college two years later, some colleges continued with a two-year course alongside the three-year course. Thus, Kesteven had a two-year course for mature or especially capable students as well as the new, longer course.

Kesteven Teacher Training College, formerly Stoke Rochford Hall, a beautiful stately home, was set in rolling parkland with a lake; a long drive led up from Stoke Rochford village, which is adjacent to the A1 and five miles south of Grantham; Roman remains have been found nearby. There has been a house on the site since the fourteenth century but the current building dates from the 1840s. Requisitioned by the War Office during WW2 it was purchased by Kesteven County Council in 1948 and used as a teacher training college until 1978.

My parents drove me there at the beginning of October 1960. I couldn't wait to get away from home and start my new life. We were met by some second-year students, one of whom relieved me of my luggage and escorted me to my designated sleeping quarters.

I left my parents without a backward glance. I

wonder what their feelings were? Were they looking forward to some peace and quiet on their own maybe, after several turbulent years? I can't imagine they were really going to miss me but I could be wrong. When my elder son went to university there was a huge hole in my life so maybe I have misjudged my parents.

Our relationship had changed by the time I went home from college. I think they were coming to terms with the fact that I was growing up. There were only a couple of times in the future that my mother became assertive again but my father still managed to be less than tactful at times, although all that was in the future.

There were several spacious rooms on the ground floor of Stoke Rochford Hall. The double main doors were rarely opened and the smaller entrance door in general use led to a corridor which went in one direction to cloakrooms and a common room and the other way to a magnificent oak-panelled hall large enough to be used as a ballroom. At one end of it was a small chamber organ and on the side facing the main doors was a grand stone fireplace in which a flower display by Mr Charity, the gardener, was often to be seen. What a delightful name! I particularly remember one Christmas just before we went down for the vacation and had an end of term ball. Mr Charity surpassed himself with an impressive display of snowdrops banked up tier on tier, filling the fireplace.

There was a series of other interconnecting rooms, used as lecture rooms, beautifully panelled and with views to the east of the college grounds.

Now I must continue to tell you about my first day at college when, having just arrived, I was taken out of the melee of new arrivals and their luggage to my room on the second floor above Matron's room on the first floor.

It was rather unfortunate that matron's room was directly underneath mine because one night during the following term when a group of us returned from a concert in Leicester I decided we needed a warm bedtime drink. However, it was against the rules to disturb people who had already gone to bed by heating up milk in the small kitchenette on our corridor. Matron stormed upstairs, possibly in her curlers and dressing gown and I received a telling off.

That wasn't all. I answered back. Oh dear, I'd been in trouble for that before and I was in trouble again. I had a severe telling off then in which I was reduced to tears. I had to go and apologise to her the next day.

Half a dozen or so rooms were up in the attics; servants' bedrooms in times gone by but female students' bedrooms now. On that first afternoon I was shown into a room with three iron beds in it. One of my room-mates was already there. Her name was Beth and she was a farmer's daughter from Rochdale. We became good friends, so much so that she was one of my bridesmaids four years later. Before long we were joined by our other roommate, Clare Le Fanu.

'Le Fanu, like deafen you,' she said as she sat on the bed when we asked her how her name was pronounced.

Clare was a lot of fun. She was two or three years older than Beth and me, had been to boarding school and spent a year studying French in Switzerland. She already had her own small car and was very independent compared with us, who had only just left home for the first time.

I was glad to get away from home but poor Beth was dreadfully homesick and I used to hear her quietly crying in bed at night.

I could not have had nicer girls as room-mates. We always got on well and are still in touch after all these years.

Beth, like me, was training to be a primary school teacher but Clare, a fluent French speaker, was going to teach in secondary schools.

Students training for secondary education studied Education, as we all did, plus two main subjects. Those of us training for Primary education studied one main subject and a range of subjects useful in primary schools like art, PE and in my case, maths.

Geography was my chosen main subject so there was a mixture of students training for primary and secondary education in the class. Unlike some colleges this was a mixed college and, because there were some older students on the course, there were mixed ages too in the lectures.

It was interesting learning alongside men and women who had been out in the world since their school days ended and had decided to follow a different career path. Some of them had been in the

Services. At the time, as I had just left school, they seemed much older but I doubt if any of them were older then forty, not so old then with hindsight! And another thing that was new was the prevalence of northern accents for many of the students came from Lancashire and Yorkshire.

After a few short weeks, it was time for our first teaching practice; time to go out to the chalk face and find out what it was all about. Of course, the world is full of people who think they know all about teaching because we've all been to school haven't we? But no, there is a lot more to teaching than that.

Our first teaching practice was for just two weeks and I went to a school in Peterborough that had been built in the Victorian era. While we were on teaching practice we had to live out of college and I was given digs with a widowed lady who lived in a cold house and was trying to earn a bit of extra money by taking in students.

This was in November, a cold foggy month and I was not very happy either with the school or my digs.

Nor was I happy with the other student who had been allocated to my school. Donald, a red headed northerner with an accent I could barely understand and a mode of slightly uncouth behaviour that didn't go down well with me or with the school. Perhaps to describe him as an ungainly youth is the best that can be said for him.

Prior to the teaching practice we had to draw up lesson plans and submit them to our tutors who, during the ensuing two weeks visited the schools to see how we were getting on and to check up on our progress with the teachers there.

I was allocated to a class of eight-year-olds and then it was time to get going. The class teacher hovered discreetly in the background keeping more than half an ear open to observe this completely green student.

I remember now standing in front of class for the very first time thinking nervously, 'This is it. Time to start.'

The rest of the week moved on. So far, so good and the feedback from my tutor and the class teacher seemed to be good.

For the second week, we again set off by coach for Peterborough, along the A1 going south and through the centre of Stamford. This road was the old Roman road called Ermine Street, later known as the Great North Road up which, in the eighteenth century the swashbuckling highwayman Dick Turpin rode. The 17th and 18th century stone buildings and the even older timber framed buildings make Stamford a very attractive place. That Autumn the narrow streets of the town were often clogged up with traffic but soon afterwards the A1 by-pass was opened, for which the residents must have been most grateful.

The time passed quickly; the end of the week arrived and so did the end of our first teaching practice.

Donald said,

'I think I did rather well there. How about you?'

Not one to be overly confident I made a noncommittal reply and we went back to college to complete our first term.

The expression on Donald's face was distinctly crestfallen a week or so later when some of us were upgraded to the two-year course, having completed a good teaching practice. Poor Donald remained on the three-year course with a somewhat dented ego.

I went home for Christmas to announce that I would be starting teaching in 1962 not 1963 as had previously been the plan. No wonder the atmosphere at home was better. I had done something right for once.

The time leading up to Christmas was occupied with working for the Royal Mail helping to deliver the Christmas post. Many students augmented their income with this job in the Christmas vacation. It involved getting up very early, snatching a quick breakfast and hot-footing in down to the mail sorting office in Selly Oak. A sack of mail for my allotted area would be emptied out onto a bench in front of me in which were many labelled pigeon holes for the different roads on my round. When the mail had been sorted into roads it had to be arranged numerically with each bundle being held together with a thick elastic band. The bundles then went into my mail bag in the right order, the mail bag went onto my back and I ventured out into the cold dawn to catch the bus to Weoley Castle, a large council estate. I was envious of the regular postmen who, having seen us on our way, stayed behind and tucked into a full English breakfast in the canteen. Tempting aromas of bacon cooking had been wafting into the sorting office for some time. The bus ride lasted for about fifteen minutes and then I started trudging round the monotonous roads of the estate.

Three incidents stand out in my memory. The first was the kindness of the elderly couple who took me into their home and gave me hot Ribena to warm me up; the second was the dog that rushed up to the letterbox inside the house as I pushed the Christmas cards through and tried to nip my fingers. I was wearing stretchy nylon gloves which the dog clamped its teeth onto and as I pulled my hands away the gloves became elongated until suddenly the animal realised its quarry had got away.

The third incident happened one day when I was waiting at the end of the round to catch the bus back to the sorting office. A thin pasty-faced looking man was also waiting for the bus. He was coughing badly and suddenly spat out blood-stained phlegm. I was horrified but probably didn't know at the time that this meant he had tuberculosis. However, I was not put off doing the job and the following year did the Christmas Post again.

In January, it was back to college again, this time travelling on one of the coaches provided for students coming from a distance away. The Birmingham bus went via Leicester and picked up students along the route.

I took advantage of my new-found independence

by using the short break in Leicester to nip off the bus and buy a packet of cigarettes. Well everyone was taking up smoking, weren't they? I thought I might as well join the crowd. My immediate group of non-smoking friends at college had more sense than I had and after smoking four of the wretched things, I decided they were so awful that I threw the packet away. A wise decision, saving myself a lifetime of addiction to nicotine, a lot of expense and possible health issues.

Life continued at college much as it had for the first term. Geography lectures given by Mr Hindley and Dr Barratt were stimulating, although I was annoyed after producing an essay for Dr Barratt, which he took weeks to mark, to be told that a Boy Scout could have done better. Oh dear!

Friendships were made and cemented with Beth, Clare, Sandra, June, Joyce; Anne, Beth's friend from Rochdale, Laurie, some second-year students and other people whose names I don't remember

Sandra had an unfortunate accident when we were playing hockey. Someone's stick contacted her mouth and came away with a few of her teeth stuck in it. Horrid. Poor Sandra.

I must have been briefly in a hockey team for I remember going to Newark to play a team from the Teachers Training College there.

In the April, it was time for our second teaching practice; mine was to be in Grimsby. So off we went again on the coach which went via Lincoln. Beth had a beautiful soprano voice and I remember as the coach approached Lincoln seeing the Cathedral silhouetted in the evening sunshine on the hill and listening to Beth's lovely rendition of 'All in an April Evening'.

This time the experience was much better, as not only was it summer time, but my digs were much more satisfactory. I was staying with a friendly family in the fishing port of Grimsby, on the bracing east coast, where the husband was a trawlerman who brought home delicious fresh fish for the family. There I ate the best fish and chips I have ever eaten.

The teaching practice went well apart from a slightly disturbing incident. We were supposed to have one or two free periods each day to evaluate our lessons, bring our notes up to date and prepare for the next day. I was approached by one of the more mature teachers who asked if I would forgo one of my free periods so that she could do something else instead of teaching the class. Bravely I stuck my neck out and said,

'Well actually no, because the college wanted us to have these times to catch up with our notes.'

'Right I'll see if someone else can fill in,' she said somewhat haughtily.

It was only later that I discovered she was the Deputy Head of the school and had I known that I would not have had the nerve to stand up to her. I discovered that she had wanted me to fill in for her while she went out to have her hair done. What a cheek. She obviously thought I was a young upstart and complained as such to a friend teaching at another school. The friend also had one of our students taking a class at that school and thus the word got around about this bolshie student. But honestly, that's the sort of thing that gets teaching a bad name, getting paid to do your job at the same time as skiving off and getting your hair done.

Eventually the teaching practice was completed satisfactorily and then it was back to college for the rest of the summer term when there was an Open Day for parents and visitors to come to the college.

Some of us had been practising country dancing for the occasion and Beth and I duly donned our rustic costumes and headscarf and pranced round the open-air theatre in bare feet on the grass.

My parents, taking advantage of my absence from home, had recently been on a rather special holiday in which they went by train to the south of France where they stayed in a luxurious hotel on the Riviera and then caught a cruise ship, en route to England from Australia. Unfortunately, there were children on the ship with chicken pox and my father took that home as a souvenir from his holiday.

Thus, they were unable to come to the open day but Auntie Louise with Uncle Doug, stepped into the breech and came in their stead. Dear Auntie Louise, always there to put herself out for others although I dare say she rather enjoyed going back to a teacher training college as it would have reminded her of the days when she was training to be a teacher.

After the end of term Uncle Len had arranged for me to work in the Income Tax offices in Birmingham for a few weeks to raise some money for a forthcoming holiday. My job was filing, when I would be given a stack of folders to sort and put away in the correct place. My father wasn't best pleased when I told him that among the files I had to sort out was the one containing his income tax details. What he earned had been a carefully guarded secret…...until then!

The middle of August arrived and it was time to set off on the aforementioned holiday which turned out to be quite an eye opener and somewhat rough and ready. I travelled to Pontefract to meet up with the other six members of a group. We were going to Scotland in an old battered van. There were three girls and four chaps. Four of the group were in the second year and would be starting teaching for real within a week or two of getting home. I was definitely the baby of the group and in fact had my nineteenth birthday the day we went climbing in the Cuillins on Skye. We were all part of the walking group at college that went off to hike in the Peak District from time to time.

We started off at the home of John, in Pontefract. He was a keen climber but was persuaded by his mother not to take a rope along with him. Probably just as well for I dread to think what I might have got involved with. We had tents with us and camped at Glen Brittle the night before we made our ascent of the highest peak on Skye called Sgurr Alasdair. It was a tough climb up into the mist and dangerous too, for right at the top you couldn't see much beyond the end of your arm and there was great potential for putting a foot out of place and hurtling to a sticky end.

We had camped in Glen Nevis on the way there and had attempted to climb Ben Nevis. I think either the weather or time defeated us.

It was an interesting holiday and broadened my horizons in more ways than one.

Chapter Seven
A Momentous Year

In October, my second year at college began and all the students who had been at college when I started had now gone on to start their teaching careers. We first-year girls moved out of the attic bedrooms in the main college buildings and went into the purpose-built halls of residence five minutes' walk away. Most of us were lucky enough to have individual study bedrooms and Clare, Beth and I had adjoining rooms on the ground floor. Just along the corridor was a kitchen where we could do our washing, ironing and prepare light meals if we chose not to eat in the college dining room. We often did this at weekends at tea time. There were three blocks and the central one had a common room for our use. One block was for the men although many of the male students lived in digs in Grantham and came in on a coach laid on by the college, every day.

Our geography studies for that year started with a week's Field Studies trip to the Gwynant Valley in Snowdonia. We stayed at the Youth Hostel at Nant Gwynant where we slept in bunk beds in dormitories and where I got told off for running a tepid bath after a hot gruelling walk. Baths could only be taken at certain times, if at all, due to hot water requirements in the kitchen.

One day we were divided into small groups and sent off to a wild area called the Cnicht to make observations. The group I was in consisted of Joyce, Meryl, me and a boy called John who seemed very easy to get on with. John remembers having to pull me out of a boggy area on that day.

In true Youth Hostel style, we had a share of the jobs to do, sweeping, washing up, peeling potatoes etc. Each day we went out to study the landscape be it to climb Snowdon or perhaps a visit to a slate mine and often repaired to a pub to refresh ourselves. At that time John, with a family background in the Plymouth Brethren, did not go into pubs.

Then it was back to college to work hard, for it was our last year at college and by this time the following year we would be launched on our careers.

Christmas was approaching and in the college choir we were singing The Childhood of Christ by Berlioz. We were practising carols too to sing at an old peoples' home in Grantham and John had acquired an old piano accordion with which to accompany us. As the cold weather came we often used to go into Grantham on a Saturday afternoon to eat toasted tea cakes at Catlins, a popular café.

Our group of friends had grown and often Barry, Geoff and the boy called John who had been on the Geography Field Course joined us. Beth, June and I had been going to a little Methodist chapel in Grantham for some time and the three boys started to go with us and John even played the organ there at times. He also could be seen and heard playing the chamber organ in the Great Hall at college. Naturally I often listened to him; John and I were becoming 'an item' to use the parlance of today.

By the time we returned to college after Christmas we were 'going out' with each other. Walking around the beautiful countryside near college was a frequent week end activity. One of our walks on a cold, frosty January day was to the place known as 'King Ludd's Grave'. I think King Ludd, if he ever existed, was a mythical figure of origin unknown. I have been unable to discover anything about him.

But John and I enjoyed the walk and I have a memory of us looking over a gate with the low winter sun behind us casting elongated shadows on the frosty grass. Often these winter walks would end with tea back in my room at college. Oh yes, bravely the college authorities had bowed to popular demand and we were at last allowed to have men in our rooms but only until six o'clock, mind you, and then they were OUT!

Nevertheless, as the warmer weather came, the quiet lanes and fields of soft grass in the countryside surrounding the college gave us plenty of opportunity to further our friendship.

As part of our course we had to write a long essay on some aspect of education for which we would be doing research over the winter and writing it during the Easter vacation. I decided to write about education and living conditions in Balsall Heath, a working class inner city area of Birmingham. The dilapidated grandeur of some of the houses showed that once it had been an affluent area but at the end of the nineteenth century many high-density small terrace houses were built. A Muslim community, started there in 1940, is now the largest in Birmingham and there are many diverse communities with residents from across the Commonwealth.

Street prostitution appeared in the 1950s and property values fell attracting Birmingham's poorer migrants. At that time many of these small homes lacked bathrooms and indoor lavatories. It was early in 1962 when I visited a school there several times and realised how these living conditions impacted on the children's education. From talking to children, staff and other people I was shocked to see how these poor migrant workers were being exploited. Ruthless landlords, not all of them white, were renting out bedding spaces to shift workers who, when their shift was over, would sleep in the space vacated by a man on a different shift.

During the Easter vacation John and I visited each other's homes for the first time. His mother had already been shown the photo of me with two other girls, that John had taken when we'd been in Snowdonia the previous autumn.

'I hope she's not the cheeky looking one,' she had apparently said. Yes, that was me. Oh dear!

I travelled up to Nottingham from Birmingham by train and John met me at Nottingham Midland Station and then we went out to his mother's flat by bus. I was feeling very nervous. It must have been daunting for her too but she had her sister-in-law, John's Auntie Elsie staying there. Quite a formidable woman I thought. No doubt after I'd gone they had a good chin wag about this slightly toffee-nosed girl.

Yes, it was true, although John and I had received a similar education, our backgrounds, especially on his mother's side were undeniably different. She lived in a council flat and came from a family of miners and had left school at thirteen. However, like my father, she'd been to night school to improve her education. She was of the same generation as my parents and that generation knew it was no good sitting around waiting for state handouts, there weren't any. If they wanted to improve their lot they had to pull themselves up by their own boot straps, as the saying goes.

Furthermore, John's father had been killed in the war and she'd had a real struggle to bring up her son singlehandedly. Her home was clean, neat and tidy but her greatest desire was to get out of the council flat and into a home of her own and she had a plan for making that happen. But more of that later.

While we waited at the station for my train back to Birmingham, to me, the space around us seemed to contract until there were just the two of us, standing in our own little world, quite apart from what was going on around us. I looked at John fondly and realised that at that very moment I had fallen in love with him. Fifty-five years later I still am.

A week later he came to visit my home and I was

very nervous again. This wasn't the bank manager's son my parents might have had in mind for me; it was a boy who lived on a council estate. Furthermore, there was the slightly worrying thought for them, of his Plymouth Brethren background. They didn't know much about the Plymouth Brethren just then, neither did I, but that was going to change.

The Brethren had been having a bad press at that time, with stories of people who'd married out of the Brethren being cast out by their families. It turned out that these stories were about the 'Closed' Brethren not the 'Open' Brethren that John's family on his father's side belonged to.

I'd probably also told them that John wouldn't go into a pub when we were in North Wales so they were no doubt wondering who on earth I'd be producing for their inspection. My parents weren't habitual drinkers of alcohol but my father did like a bottle of wine at Christmas or when he was out for a meal.

To make things worse, poor John had fallen off his bike the previous week and his face looked a mess. None of this boded well.

However, the visit was a success and when John accepted the glass of cider that Dad offered him things started to look up.

Soon after that we went back to college for our last term before we qualified as teachers. There was another teaching practice, in Grimsby again, for me.

So again, on Sunday evenings the coaches were waiting in front of the college to carry us off to the places our chosen schools were in, farewells were said and they loaded up and rolled off, one after the other down the long college drive and onto the Great North Road. John's coach took him south with the group of students going to Northampton whilst mine rolled northwards towards Grimsby.

The last time I'd been in Grimsby I hadn't been in love but this time I was and I missed John a lot. I had digs in Cleethorpes in a guest house there just across the road from the beach. Acker Bilk's music, 'Stranger on the Shore' was popular at the time and I used to wander on Cleethorpes's beach longing to be with my beloved, with that haunting tune going through my mind. Whenever I hear it today my mind is cast back to that time.

The teaching practice passed off satisfactorily. I was in a nice modern single-story school with friendly staff. The class sizes of forty-eight were unacceptably large by today's standards but the children were well-behaved and I don't remember it being regarded as a big problem. Just a lot of hard work.

My class teacher had a friend in another school and when the friend had a day off they decided to play a joke on me. The friend posed as an HMI, one of Her Majesty's Inspectors, and came to 'inspect' me, armed with horn-rimmed glasses and an important looking folder. The two friends walked round the classroom together and no doubt had a good giggle in the corner when the 'Inspector' was ostensibly examining the children's work. I was completely taken in by the joke.

They must have thought I could cope with a bit of teasing. I did.

Back at college there were end of term exams and then it was nearly time to go home, await our results and start on our teaching careers. But just before then my parents came to college to collect my luggage and objects that I had accumulated in my time there. John joined us and we all had lunch at the Ram Jam Inn on the A1 just south of Colsterworth. They were beginning to realise that my relationship with him was serious.

While my mother helped me with some packing Dad and John went to Grantham in the car. Dad had a rather nice maroon Singer Vogue saloon car at the time and decided that if John, who'd passed his driving test the previous year, was going to be driving me around in the future he wanted to know what sort of driver he was. He invited John to take the wheel and take the car for a short drive. That apparently went alright but before they returned to college he said to John,

'You don't know what you're taking on with this girl. She was a terrible teenager. You have been warned.'

I've mentioned before that my parents had little experience of teenage girls and in the light of what we experienced later, they got off lightly! But I think again Dad was showing his lack of sensitivity. He had a habit of doing that.

So there we are. End of story. I was now grown up and about to go out into the world.

32. Susie in 1960

33. Kesteven Teacher Training College

34. Country dancing on Open Day

35. Susie on her nineteenth birthday in the Cuillins on Skye

36. Susie with friends at Nant Gwynant Youth Hostel, Snowdonia

37. Susie and John at college 1962

38. Susie in the college grounds 1962

Chapter Eight
No, of Course it isn't the End

I'd had a wonderful time at college. I'd escaped the strictures of home. Hardly ever again did my parents seem as overbearing as they had in my earlier years. I'd had some interesting experiences, I'd really enjoyed spending so much time in the country but more than anything else I'd fallen deeply in love.

John and I walked together down the drive for the last time and caught the bus into Grantham. We caught the train to Nottingham and then at the Midland Station, where I had fallen in love with him a few months earlier, he kissed me goodbye and put me on the Birmingham train and that was that. The future was a blank.

I sat on the train as it rattled down the track and cried. Would I ever see him again?

I had applied to the City of Birmingham Education Office in Margaret Street for a teaching job in Birmingham. There was a severe shortage of teachers at the time in the city, partly because fewer teachers were coming out of college that year due to the course having been lengthened to three years but it was also due to Birmingham being an unpopular place in which to teach.

I had a brief interview; there seemed to be little

doubt that they would offer me a job. But where would it be?

'Which school would you like to teach in?' I was unexpectedly asked.

'Green Meadow Junior School please,' was the answer. I'd been looking at the map to locate possible schools not too far away from home. Green Meadow was perfect. Not only was it a modern building but it was within easy walking distance of home. There had been no thoughts in my mind of teaching anywhere other than in my home town.

My wish was granted and I was very pleased that I had not been allocated to an inner-city school. Dad drove me up there one evening so that we could have a look at the place where I would be working for the foreseeable future. The two-storey building was set among playgrounds and green fields in an area of modern housing. There was a caretaker's house on the site and as we walked through the gates the man came out and approached us to see who these invaders of his territory might be.

'Leave this to me,' Dad said, expecting trouble.

Suddenly the two men started grinning at each other and shook hands.

My father said,

'Well I never, is that really you Old Nick?'

'Yes, it is indeed Mr Williams, sir. I haven't seen you since the end of the war.'

It turned out that Nick had been caretaker of another nearby school where my mother had been in charge of the First Aid post during the war. So far from being flung off the school site as trespassers we were welcomed and had a good look round.

I soon realised that this school and its catchment area of owner occupied homes was very different from Balsall Heath, the area I had studied for my long essay. And that the children from the two areas had a very unequal start in life.

In my two years at the Green Meadow Junior School I always felt Nick was keeping an eye on this young teacher and yes, I was young. Today's teachers take a three-year degree course and then a one-year PGCE, Post Graduate Course in Education, unless the whole lot is combined but in any case, it will be four years of training. With my birthday being at the end of August I was barely twenty when I stepped into the classroom for the first time as a qualified teacher.

It had been arranged that as soon as I left college, which was a few weeks before the Birmingham schools finished for the summer holiday, I would go to teach in one of the city schools. I went off by bus each morning to a school at Yardley and had a few weeks trying out my newly acquired teaching skills; useful before I started the real thing in September.

John and I exchanged letters and after the end of the school term I was invited to go up to Nottingham and stay with him and his mother for a couple of days.

We were overjoyed to see each other again. The future was not looking blank after all. Within a few days we had decided we wanted to spend the rest of our lives together.

I went home to Birmingham with a spring in my step and after I had gone John told his mother that we would be getting engaged. She was crestfallen and most unhappy. Her plan for getting off a council estate and owning a home of her own had been that as John would be earning a salary as a teacher, she would put down the deposit on a house and he would be able to pay the mortgage. For this end, she had been saving hard for years out of her small income. Now her dream was gone.

My parents also had to resign themselves to the news that the boy from the council estate was going to become my husband and I would be leaving home for good. Marriage to the bank manager's son was definitely off!

A few weeks later John would be coming to stay; the main purpose being to ask my father's permission to marry his daughter. Yes, people still sometimes did that

In the meantime, Beth came down to Birmingham and we set off on a walking holiday on the Welsh Borders. We went by train to Hereford and stayed in Youth Hostels and walked along canal tow paths and country tracks. All the time I was bursting to tell Beth my secret that John and I were soon to become engaged. The last place we stayed in was Crickhowell, not far from Abergavenny and then it was back home. We went by train to Worcester where we had arranged to meet my father who was there on business for the day and then home to await John's imminent arrival.

Fortunately, the awaited permission to marry was a foregone conclusion but we agreed not to get formally engaged until December.

My twentieth birthday followed soon after this and then before long it was time to go into school to get ready for my teaching career to begin.

I taught at Green Meadow Junior School for two years until we got married. I could not have had a better school in which to teach to begin my career. The classes were streamed with three classes in each year. I was given the A stream, a class of forty-two children. I had a bright, airy classroom upstairs and the children, with barely an exception, were well-behaved and a pleasure to teach.

Those were the days when teaching was formal and the teacher's word was law not only with the pupils but with the parents too. The desks were in rows so all eyes faced the front, not in groups, as they were later, when it was all too easy for the little dears to catch the eye of a classmate and get distracted.

The timetable was well regulated and everyone knew where they were.

I was fully supported by Mr Davenport, the excellent head teacher. The only other teacher I remember from that time was Renee Dowler, possibly in her forties then, who was kind to me and whose home at Rubery I visited. Among other things she oversaw distributing the materials for sewing lesson. I remember the 'binca', canvas material and coloured threads for making little mats which provided the opportunity to practise several embroidery stitches. I even went on a course to improve my teaching of sewing.

After that we progressed to making green gingham sewing cases with a strip of the material cut on the cross to use as a binding round the edge, more embroidery on the cover and a soft material inside to stick pins and needles into. I don't remember the boys being taught sewing; maybe they went off and did woodwork with one of the male teachers. Probably we didn't have equal opportunities then for the different sexes.

I taught all the subjects on the curriculum but when it came to games lessons and football, of which I had no knowledge whatsoever, I used to say,

'Off you go boys, get yourselves organised and I'll come over from time to time and see how you are getting on'. It seemed to work.

I was inspected during that probationary year by a genuine HMI inspector and all was well.

I took my class on a trip to Malvern where we went to British Camp and the children enjoyed running up and down the huge embankments. I don't remember now what the educational aspect of the trip was but it could have been studying an ancient settlement in England with some Geography thrown in as the Malvern Hills are volcanic. In any case there was a fabulous view from the top over to the Welsh Hills.

As well as teaching, we all had to do playground duty once a week and dinner duty too.

Playground duty meant going out to ring the bell or blow the whistle for the children to come into school in the morning and at the beginning of the afternoon and to go out there with your cup of coffee at morning break for twenty minutes. That was when you were still allowed to stand out there among the children with a cup of hot coffee. Later it was deemed too dangerous in case it got spilt on them.

Once when I was out there with a happy bunch of children gathered round me one of them suddenly said,

'Oh, look Miss, what's that on your shoulder?' I glanced down and there was huge spider. What a joke it was when I shrieked at the plastic spider one of the little dears had put there. I was the one who had hot coffee spilt on her then.

Having to do playground duty was something I had nightmares about long after I retired from teaching. I'd be sitting in the staff room enjoying a coffee when suddenly I'd remember I was supposed to be out there keeping an eye on two hundred or so children and sending for help if there was an accident. I'd rush out there, in my dream, and hope no one had noted my absence.

I only remember one girl who was a bit of a problem in my first class. Her name was Lynda and she had red hair. Throughout my two years at the school Lynda was at times, quite frankly, a pain in the neck. Strange to say though, at the end of my time there, on the last afternoon she was the one who hung back after all the other children had left and burst into tears.

'I wish you wasn't leaving Miss,' she said.

How extraordinary I thought to myself. I had felt she was the one child who would be glad to see me go. Afterwards I concluded that yet again we don't know what is going on in other people's minds. I think maybe her home life was not as happy as one imagined it to be and that her time in my class had provided her with a sense of security.

Making the classroom look attractive was very important but it took a lot of time. Some of that was done before each term started when I went into school and put up pictures of what we were learning about. As the term progressed I'd put up displays of the children's work; that made them feel valued. They liked to have their work displayed especially at Parents' Evenings. It had to be done neatly with suitable backing paper. There's quite an art to making a classroom look good.

I could do my lesson preparation at home. Reading up about what I was teaching, making charts and diagrams and writing yearly, termly, weekly and daily lesson plans took several hours each week. My father used to hover in the back ground when I was still working at ten o'clock in the evening. I did most of my marking at school either at lunch time or after school. There was no way I'd be carrying home three or more sets of books when there were more than forty children in the class.

The relationship with my mother showed a marked improvement in those two years I lived at home and taught nearby. She seemed at last to realise I had grown up and knew what I was talking about and she enjoyed sitting down with me when I returned from school and listening to how my day had gone.

Looking back that was only one of two times I felt we'd really got on well together. The other was when I was a small child and we wandered on country footpaths together when we stayed at the farm and she taught me the names of wild flowers and butterflies and read stories to me.

I feel a deep sadness when friends talk of the loving relationship they have had with their mothers. Why couldn't mine have been like that? In later years she slipped into dementia and the time for any meaningful relationship was gone.

John and I were finding it hard being apart. For that first year of our engagement we saw each other once a fortnight when we went to stay at each other's homes alternately. I slept in John's bedroom and he slept on a camp bed in the living room.

His mother was not happy. She was finding it very difficult to come to terms with the fact that she would be committed to staying in her council flat and not moving to her own home as had been her plan. The poor lady saw me as the one who had spoilt her dream.

With hindsight, I have a great deal of sympathy for her but of course that wasn't the way I felt at the time. I just didn't understand. She'd lost her husband, she was now losing her son and her hopes of owning her own home were thwarted.

During the Autumn we had been to see Uncle Stan in Birmingham's famous Jewellery Quarter where he made diamond rings. I wish I'd known then that my natural grandfather, Evan Charles Voyce, had also been a jeweller and had made diamond rings somewhere in the same vicinity but that was a long time before I delved into the history of my birth family.

I doubt if Uncle Stan's workshop with its peg benches and cramped quarters in the mid twentieth century was substantially different from Evan Charles Voyce's at the end of the nineteenth century.

It was quite extraordinary the way the Jewellery Quarter had changed from the days when it was a wealthy residential district with substantial Georgian houses. From the late 1700s manufacturing businesses began to be established despite it being a residential area. The middle classes began to move out and large factories and workshops were constructed for goldsmiths and silversmiths. As the Jewellery Quarter became even more important workshops and small factories were built in what had once been the gardens of the large Georgian properties.

Uncle Stan's workshop may have been one such place, as to find it we went down the side of what must have once been a large house. We climbed an outside staircase and met Uncle Stan at the top. He took us inside and measured my ring finger and asked us what sort of design we had in mind.

We thought three stones with the centre one slightly larger than the other two would be good. He arranged several sizes of stones on black velvet and then he and John had a private conversation about the price. I'm quite sure that he was offering us preferential prices but even so there was a limit to John's budget. Eventually the business was dealt with and in due course the ring was finished and was sent to John in Nottingham to await our formal engagement. He told me only recently that when it arrived his mother showed no interest in it at all. Her attitude must have been very disappointing for him.

We had arranged to get engaged on the 15th December 1962 and to have a celebratory meal out in the evening. John and his mother travelled by train from Nottingham to Birmingham. When I went to meet them at New Street Station I was alarmed by the announcement that I heard over the Public Address system.

'Will Miss Williams please go to the Station Master's Office.'

Whatever had happened, I wondered as I hurried up the steps to his office. No need to be alarmed, I was told, it was just a delay. The engine for their train had been 'lost' when they needed to change trains at Derby.

An hour later they arrived and we travelled to my home in Selly Oak. My mother took John's mother under her wing and they had a heart to heart chat while we went off somewhere on our own. My mother, despite her other faults, was good at talking to people or perhaps was a good listener or both. I can remember occasions when I came home from school and was confronted on more than one occasion by a woman who showed by her tear-stained face that she had been unburdening herself of her woes to my mother.

I was told afterwards that tears had been shed by John's mother. This was her first visit to my home and she may have felt awkward being in more affluent surroundings but in any case, she was very unhappy about our engagement. She had repeatedly told John she didn't approve of the engagement and couldn't understand why he wanted to get married. I knew she was unhappy but he hid the worst of her feelings from me.

Before we went out in the evening John presented me with the three-stone diamond ring that Uncle Stan had made, the diamonds sparkled and the gold glittered and I was very happy. We went to a restaurant at Stourbridge and as we rarely went out for a meal in those days it was a very special occasion.

I spent that first Christmas of our engagement at John's home where Auntie Grace and Uncle Alf joined us.

Auntie Grace, John's mother's sister, was born in 1892 and lived until 1981; Uncle Alf was their brother. They lived in Hyson Green in a row of terrace houses built for the workers at the nearby Players Cigarette factory at the end of the 1800s. Auntie Grace was the eldest of four sisters and two brothers, raised in a house with a lavatory down the yard and a cold tap in the scullery. In the living-room there was an open fire on which, in the past, before a gas cooker was installed in the scullery, the cooking had been done and in front of which on the weekly bath night the tin bath would be placed after it had been brought up from the coal cellar.

On bath night a fire was lit under the copper in the corner of the scullery and jugs of hot water would be brought in. The entire family used the same water starting with mother, then the girls and the boys and finally the father. Like many eldest girls in the families of her generation Auntie Grace was the one who remained unmarried and, as the parents grew old, cared for them until they died.

But there had been a complication in this family because Uncle Alf had severe learning difficulties, never learnt to read and write and didn't go out to work. Auntie Grace cared for him all her life, forsaking marriage and children of her own.

Quite frankly he was a bit of a shock to me as I found his speech almost unintelligible and his table manners were, as you would expect, not highly polished. But once again with hindsight I applaud Auntie Grace for not hiding him away but continuing to care for him in the family home.

I have to admit that the difference between this house and my own was very great. I had grown accustomed to a three-bedroomed centrally heated house with wall to wall carpets, a bathroom and separate toilet and another toilet downstairs, a telephone and television, to a dining table covered with a clean cloth, set with matching china and attractive cutlery, to a kitchen well-appointed and with every convenience including a fridge and a washing machine.

Auntie Grace loved good china and sparkling cut glass; and when she came to tea after we were married she lovingly polished mine when she helped with the washing up. She just didn't have any of her own and made do with mismatching plates and cutlery.

Much later when she died she left quite a substantial amount of money to her nieces and nephew for which no doubt every one of her beneficiaries was grateful but I couldn't help wishing she had used some of it to buy for herself the pretty things she so obviously liked and which would have made her own life more comfortable.

39. Susie and her parents 1960

40. John and Susie Easter 1962

*41. Miss Susie Williams at Green Meadow Junior School
1964*

42. 'Miss' with her class 1964

Chapter Nine
Hard Times

The winter of 1962-63 has gone down in the memories of people who were alive at the time as one of the longest and severest winters on record. From Boxing Day until March 6th there was frost every day and from the end of December until March there was snow on the ground with huge drifts in places. Transport was disrupted, people had to walk to work and food supplies ran low. There was frost on the inside of windows making beautiful patterns of ferns; dish cloths by kitchen sinks froze overnight. The way people pulled together and helped each other was reminiscent of the wartime spirit.

For me it meant that my walk to school was more difficult and slippery than normal but what was worse was that it meant the children couldn't go out into the playground for nine weeks. One or two days of wet playtimes was bad enough but nine weeks when the children couldn't get out and let off steam made life in the classroom very difficult. It also meant the teachers lost their break as well.

This was at a time when small boys wore short trousers until they were eleven and similarly girls wore short skirts. Legs were cold, often knees were chapped and chilblains were common.

John and I continued see each other once a

fortnight, travelling by train and bus to each other's homes. John was teaching at secondary school in Nottingham and despite the awful weather that winter, we often went walking in the Peak District in Derbyshire with a group of children from his school. Up there the snow lay thickly, blanketing the fields and moorland and there were deep drifts against the stone walls.

I particularly remember one walk over exposed ground where I wondered what the bits of wood were that stuck out of the ground. Eventually I realised that they were the tops of gate posts and was amazed that we were walking that far above ground. There was a thick crust of ice on top of the snow but every so often it gave way and one would plunge into a deep hole. We walked eleven miles that day in those very arduous conditions.

We wrote to each other every week and there was the occasional phone call although that was fraught with difficulty. To phone me, John had to go out to use a public phone box for which one had to have the correct coins. There was a sequence of pressing buttons A and B and putting your money in at the right time or getting your money back if the phone wasn't answered. I didn't need to do it very often so the exact procedure eludes me after all these years.

Alternatively, you could go via the operator and ask for the charges to be reversed. The operator dialled the number you wanted and when the phone was answered, asked the person at the other end if they would accept the call. Hopefully they would. If you did that on a long distance call the pips went after three minutes which kept a check on how much was being spent on the call.

We must have done that sometimes but there were to be no lengthy, private and loving chats between us as my wretched father would be standing by my side ready to cut us off when the pips went. Three minutes was all that he allowed me and three minutes was no time at all to be connected to one's beloved; under the eagle eye of my father it was very stressful.

What with John's mother muttering in her bedroom when I was staying there about this engagement she didn't want to be happening and my father denying us the privacy of a decent chat on the phone I began to wonder how our relationship could continue.

I told John it was only fair that he should come to my home for the second Christmas of our engagement. However, when he said he couldn't leave his mother the following Christmas I felt I had to put my foot down.

'Either you come to my home this Christmas or we break off our engagement,' I said. John always cared for his mother but I felt that if he was going to marry me, sometimes I should come first.

In the end his mother spent Christmas at her flat with Auntie Grace and Uncle Alf. John came to Birmingham for Christmas.

Our relationship was further tested as the time for

our wedding approached when my mother went into her assertive persona again. During a weekend spent in Nottingham we would have made certain decisions about wedding arrangements or whatever, but by the following weekend when I had spent the week under her influence he would find my mother had been bringing pressure to bear on me and I had changed my mind. The poor chap didn't know where he was. But all that was sometime in the future as during the summer holiday we went to stay with his Auntie Beth at Llanfairfechan in North Wales.

Auntie Beth and her friend Auntie Kath had both been district nurses at Stone in Staffordshire. When they retired they bought a house at Llanfairfechan right by the sea. They had permanent tenants in the flat on the ground floor and they occupied the remaining three floors, possibly having a flat each, I don't remember. There was still loads of room and they often had people to stay.

Obviously, we didn't share a bedroom. Oh, my goodness me, no! Auntie Beth, like the rest of John's father's side of the family, were Plymouth Brethren and there were strict rules about pre-marriage behaviour but in any case, this was in pre-contraceptive pill days and one had to be very careful.

I remembered that my father had threatened that if I got pregnant before we were married I would be thrown out. I believe he really would have done that or at the very least there would have been a quick marriage and that wouldn't have suited our plans at all.

But we had a wonderful fortnight at Llanfairfechan when we could forget about the difficulties of having to spend so much time apart and we could enjoy our time alone together. We both liked hiking and there were the mountains of Snowdonia rising behind the village of Llanfairfechan. One day we did a huge twenty-five-mile hike right up Carnedd Llewellyn, a mountain almost as high as Snowdon. There were other less ambitious hikes as well.

One day we went across to the Isle of Mann on the ferry. We also visited Llandudno where we joined a crowd that had gathered on the promenade to see what would happen to a car that had been on the beach and had somehow become submerged by the sea. Some men had a rope attached to it and were trying to get it out of the water. Quite a crowd had gathered to watch. I felt something touch my ankle and turned around, surprised to see that it was the hem of a nun's habit. She had felt as curious as everybody else.

We went to Llanfairfechan on another occasion when an aunt of John's had come over from Canada with her husband and they were staying with Auntie Beth. John hired a car in Nottingham, stayed the night in Birmingham, from where we set off early in the following morning to reach North Wales.

Near Llangollen we looked down at the mysterious scene of the valleys filled with early morning mist. When we arrived at Llanfairfechan Auntie Beth's sister Ruth was there with her husband Charley, a very strict Plymouth Brother.

We had just arrived when he looked at me in my trousers and made a sanctimonious comment, possibly a biblical quotation, about it being shameful for a woman to wear men's apparel. It did not endear him to me.

Shortly afterwards Auntie Kath came up to me.

'I always wear trousers when I go walking on the mountains,' she said. 'Take no notice of him.' So I didn't. Silly man.

We went back to Birmingham the next day and then John returned home to Nottingham.

My mother took me to London for a few days of mother and daughter bonding. But it didn't work. We went shopping, I loved Liberty's, we went to Madame Tussauds and we probably went to the Royal Albert Hall for a Promenade concert. Why didn't it work? I don't know but every day there was some awkwardness. I just didn't want her to dominate me. Such a shame really. You'd have thought we could have got on like good chums just for a few days.

In August 1963, it was my twenty-first birthday and my parents held a party to celebrate the occasion. It was held at the Dame Elizabeth Cadbury Hall in Bourneville. I was delighted that my friends from college, Beth and Clare, could come. They stayed with neighbours just across the road from where we lived.

As well as delicious buffet food there was dancing. It was a happy gathering of friends and relations. Uncle Percy proposed a toast to me, the birthday girl and turned it into a good wishes speech for our engagement as well, although we had by now been engaged for several months.

That Autumn we decided that spending a fortnight between visits was just too long so we decided to visit each other weekly. But we also decided it was too expensive to carry on using the train. We started to use the Midland Red X99 bus. This was cheaper than the train but the journey, via Tamworth and Ashby-de-la-Zouch, took longer.

We'd go home from school on the Friday evening, have a meal and then start the four-hour door to door journey. For whichever one of us whose turn it was to travel that week- end it meant eight hours in total on the road. But it was worth it.

We were now into the second year of our engagement and were saving up hard to buy our first home. John had found out that there were new houses being built at Rise Park near Bulwell in Nottingham and we worked out that we could just afford to buy one, especially if we went without a honeymoon and used the money we had put aside for that as a deposit on the house. The alternative was to rent a top floor flat in one of the old houses on the Mansfield Road. The brand new three-bed roomed detached house on the edge of the countryside was much more appealing.

Money was a problem; there was a shortage of it and we had to work out how to make a little go a long way. John decided that he would make some of our furniture. Auntie Grace had a spare bedroom in her house at Hyson Green and she allowed John to use it as a workshop. He cycled down there almost every night after school and made a dining table, four chairs, a sideboard and a lovely dressing table for me with a long mirror down one side. He had been to a local timber yard, selected a teak log which was then sawn into planks at the yard and delivered to Auntie Grace's house.

Danish style furniture was very popular at the time and when I'd been staying for the week-end in Nottingham we'd been to a furniture shop called Hopewell's to get some ideas on the design we liked.

When we had a week-end together at my home we usually went into town to look round the shops and to get ideas for the things we wanted in our new home. We enjoyed going in to Rackham's and looking at all the things we couldn't possibly afford to buy. Further along Corporation Street there was a furniture store called Maples but, beautiful though it was, the style of furniture in there seemed heavy and old fashioned.

If we could afford it we went to the Ceylon Tea Centre nearby for lunch. They had an interesting array of salads that you could choose from at a salad bar and they did delicious Rum Babas for dessert.

Chapter Ten
Onward

John had been influenced in his choice of career by his Auntie Win, born in 1910. She was one of the three children of James and Elizabeth Howell and had two brothers, Joe, born in 1913 and Douglas, born in 1916.

Auntie Win became a teacher and by the time I knew her she was head of an infant school in Ipswich. She still had connections with Nottingham as the family had lived there for many years from the 1920s onward and had been active members of the Brethren Meeting at Clumber Hall.

It was from Clumber Hall that her brother Douglas and his wife Marjorie went out as missionaries to the Near East after WW2.

During the war her brother Joe, John's father, was killed in Hong Kong on Christmas Day 1941. Win and her mother, still living in Nottingham, were very supportive to his mother, both when her husband went away to war and after he was killed. John's mother continued to attend Clumber Hall but as he became older John attended a Brethren meeting nearer to his home at Broxtowe.

We both had a Christian upbringing but I felt my broad beliefs nurtured in the Congregational Church did not sit well with the Brethren narrower beliefs and as John was starting to move away from the Brethren we went to a Baptist Church on Sunday morning when I was staying in Nottingham.

I had been to church membership classes at Carrs Lane when I was in my late teens but in all honesty, I found myself unable to make a commitment to the church; I just did not fully believe.

However, not long after I left college I was invited to go to a missionary conference at the Hayes Conference Centre at Swanick in Derbyshire. I don't know why I agreed to go as I have quite mixed feelings about missionaries who, in the past, have been insensitive towards the 'primitive' people they have gone to convert. Today, not only do they give help with agriculture and medicine among other things but are more sympathetic to the communities they find.

So, there I was at Swanick listening to the experiences of missionaries who were home on furlough. They talked about their daily lives; some of them were facing incredible dangers; they talked about the people they were working among and why they were there.

During one speech I was absolutely riveted by what the speaker was saying and I suddenly realised that Christianity wasn't about the details of what you believed. It was about love and how you lived your life and how you followed the teaching of Jesus. I suddenly understood what it was all about. Soon after that I became a member of Carrs Lane Church.

Women had long been accepted into the Ministry in the Congregational Church but were not even permitted to speak in Brethren meetings other than in meetings solely for women. Neither, of course, were women ordained in the Church of England until comparatively recent years. I believe strongly that all people, regardless of their gender and race are equal in the sight of God and should be able to serve equally in the churches they attend.

I also objected to having to wear a hat when I went to Brethren meetings on a Sunday morning. I was not in agreement with their Fundamentalist ideas. Saint Paul had pronounced two thousand years ago that women should keep their heads covered in church so Brethren ladies wore hats but then to be fair that was also true of ladies in the Church of England and many other churches at the time. St Paul's ideas were part of society at his time and were relevant then. But we've moved on.

Such a lot has changed, women are now ordained, hardly anyone wears a hat to church and there are even discussions going on about whether the Church of England should allow same sex marriages in church.

We did occasionally go to Clumber Hall and I think it must have been on one of those occasions that I first met Auntie Win who was visiting Nottingham.

She would have been in her early fifties at that time and was headmistress of an infant school in Ipswich. I came to be very fond of her over the years and admired her greatly for the way she cared for her own mother, for the support she gave John's mother and for the time she gave to her brother's children when they were at boarding school while their parents were abroad.

However, she terrified me on that first meeting. I wish I could remember her exact words but having looked me up and down in true school ma'am fashion, she made some sort of comment about my training being a waste of time as I was shortly to be married and would be leaving the profession when I had children. That was me duly squashed! As a very young teacher I was still very much in awe of headteachers.

Again, with hindsight I don't think that was her intention at all but in a way, it was perhaps a fair comment. And after all it was then only twenty years since women had been obliged to give up their teaching careers when they married. And still in the 1960s most women stopped work when they had children. Here I can say, yet again, that there have been many changes in my lifetime.

I wonder if there was also a touch of irony here. I think at one time there was a man in her life but the romance, if there was one, came to nothing. There was even a hint that Auntie Beth might have had something to do with its demise.

We were soon into 1964, the year of our marriage and there were arrangements to be made. We had decided to be married at my local parish church of St Mary's in Selly Oak. It might have been expected that I would get married at the church I was currently attending but faced with the choice of being married in the centre of Birmingham opposite Marks and Spencer's on a busy Saturday morning in August or at an attractive church at the end of a tree lined drive with plenty of parking space, the choice was quite simple.

Much nearer the time we had a pre-wedding meeting with the Vicar, Rev. Michael Webster. He was happy to marry us despite not being members of his congregation; I did of course live in the parish so we had a legal right to be married there. Slightly embarrassed, he skirted round the possibility of planning our family and seemed most relieved when I said I had already been to the Family Planning Clinic.

The pill was not an option at that time and unless the new bride wanted to leave the 'arrangements' to her husband she went along to the Family Planning Clinic somewhere near Five Ways and got fitted with a Dutch Cap and was given a tube of lubricating jelly. Strangely the friend with whom I went became pregnant on her honeymoon and I wasn't far behind.

The Dame Elizabeth Cadbury Hall had proved to be very satisfactory for my 21st birthday party so that was booked again for the wedding reception.

The invitations were printed and sent out and wedding presents started to arrive. John's mother gave us a beautiful Wedgewood dinner service; my parents bought us a double bed and Uncle Percy and Auntie Madge gave us a most extensive set of saucepans made in Uncle's factory. There were sherry glasses and Stuart crystal wine glasses, cutlery, casseroles, towels and bedlinen and many other gifts. People were most kind and generous.

Beth and Judith had agreed to be my bridesmaids. They wore simple short dresses of blue Broderie Anglaise.

My wedding dress had been made for me and was white brocade in a slim fitted style. I'd been into town with my mother and we'd chosen the material together. I was very slim at the time and when we had stayed with Auntie Beth the previous year she had said she thought I was too thin. I had a fine net veil held in place by a simple headdress.

My bouquet was golden freesias and white roses. Auntie Madge kindly offered to do the flowers in church and the blue delphiniums and other flowers looked beautiful. Well I'm sure they did but I don't remember looking at them. I was far too happy and excited on the day.

John and his mother had come down from Nottingham the day before in the little Ford car John had hired for our honeymoon in Scotland.

Oh yes, we did have a honeymoon after all because my father said we must have a honeymoon and lent us the £200 to pay for it. We promised to pay him back as soon as possible and to that end put something aside each month.

Auntie Win had driven over from Ipswich but her mother, John's Grandma, was too frail to make the journey. Later we were delighted to see a photo of her dressed up in what she would have worn had she been able to come to the wedding.

This was in the days when telegrams were still sent to the happy couple at weddings and were read out by the best man. Grandma had sent us a telegram wishing us great happiness and God's richest blessings. Now fifty-three years later, I can say that indeed we have been richly blest.

Friends and relations made their way to the church. A coach was hired to transport John's Nottingham relations and friends to the wedding. Among them was one of his mother's sisters, Auntie Elizabeth, who had come over with her husband, Uncle Ern, from Canada. Worryingly the coach was delayed and they only just arrived in time, in the rain.

John and his best man, a colleague called Alan, were already at the church and the side of the aisle for the bride's friends and relations was packed but hardly anyone was on the groom's side. Where could they be? They arrived with minutes to spare and scurried down the long church drive and seated themselves.

Back at my home the wedding cars arrived, the first taking my mother and the bridesmaids to the church and then me and my father.

Hurrying along the church drive just as we arrived was a little old lady who lived a few doors down the hill from our house. Her name was Miss Williams, just as mine was. I insisted that we sat in the car for another minute or two to let her go into church first. She would still be a maiden lady when she came out of church but I would be a married woman.

The photographers had arrived and the cameras were clicking. My mother looked very attractive in a gold coloured dress and jacket with matching hat. Unfortunately, there was a bandage round her ankle as she had fallen down a step and sprained it a few days before. The bridesmaids looked very pretty in their pale blue dresses and the photo of me and my father walking into church showed him to be a very proud father. Everything was going very well.

As we walked down the aisle I was just amazed to see how full the church was. There were the friends and relations who had been invited to the wedding and reception afterwards. I particularly remember Auntie Louise who turned around and gave me a happy smile.

There were neighbours who had come to see the wedding of the girl they had watched growing up. Even children were there who until recently had been in my class. It made me so happy to see all these people who had come to wish us well.

But most of all, standing by the altar steps, was the man I was deeply in love with and this was the day we would be promising to love each other 'in sickness and in health until death us do part'.

After the ceremony as we emerged into the church porch the bells were ringing and we couldn't stop smiling. We were married at last. More photos were taken and then it was time to set off for the reception but there was one important port of call on the way.

Uncle Walter and Auntie Flo, the quiet loving Quaker couple that my parents had known for years, had moved to a bungalow in Bourneville when Uncle retired from his job at the cemetery. He had died two years before our wedding so Auntie Flo was on her own and by now was a very frail old lady. I had continued to visit her from time to time and she left a deep impression on me.

She couldn't get to the wedding but longed to see me on my wedding day so we arranged that, on our way to the reception nearby, we would stop and see her. She came to her front door and the door of the limousine was opened so she could see us and to call out her good wishes. I didn't get out of the car because managing my dress would have been difficult but I rather wish I had and had gone to give her a hug. What does a little difficulty with a dress matter when the important issue is to make a dear old lady happy.

Then it was on to the reception and more photographs. The drizzle had stopped and the sun came out and photographs were taken on the sweeping lawns that surrounded the Hall.

It is customary at weddings to take photographs of the wedding guests, of the friends and relations but I was adamant that this would not happen at our wedding. I felt my mother's family would be vying for position and I wasn't going to have any of that. I deeply regret that now because I dare say I was over sensitive about it. What a wonderful historical record it would have been of people who are no longer alive. In fact, apart from my cousin Mary, my two bridesmaids Beth and Judith and our college friend Clare and ourselves, everyone has passed away.

However, several photos were taken by people who had taken their own cameras and so there is a partial record of the people who came to our wedding.

John and I were blissfully happy and I smiled so much that my face was aching but John's mother was not happy and there were tears. What she had been dreading for the two years of our engagement had now happened. Her son now belonged to another woman and she was on her own.

The reception was held and everyone sat down to lunch. The cake was cut, speeches were made, toasts were drunk and then it was time for me to get changed into my going away outfit, a blue dress and jacket and matching hat and off we went in the hired car.

Our luggage had been hidden away, back at my parents' home so we went there first to collect it. As John stowed it in the car I found the packet of confetti I had hidden away and sprinkled it all around the house, in beds, in drawers, in fact everywhere. I don't suppose my mother was best pleased when she returned, to find that her beautifully clean and tidy house, specially prepared for visitors, was now covered in confetti. Whatever was I thinking of? I think it was in my mind that it would be a sort of joke. I can just imagine Auntie Glad and Uncle Len, who had come up from Bournemouth for the wedding on getting into bed that night.

Auntie Glad would have said in horror,

'Oh Bab, look what she's done.'

And my poor mother, or maybe my father, would have had to get the dustpan and brush and clear up the mess. And then they'd find some in their own bed too. And that was after getting out of the cutlery drawers from among the knives, fork and spoons.

But by then we were on our way to the Lake District where we were spending the first night of our honeymoon.

So now I am a married woman. I must be grown up by now although the confetti incident probably shows I wasn't so I'd better go on a bit further.

43. Wedding Day August 8th, 1964

44. Susie with her parents

45. Some of my pupils joining in with throwing confetti

46. John with his mother

47. Auntie Win

48. Grandma Howell in her wedding outfit

49. John and his mother looking at what will be our first home

50. Our home at Rise Park, Nottingham

51. With my class at Berridge Road School, Nottingham

Chapter Eleven
What Happened Next

It was a long way to the Lake District from Birmingham on that wet Saturday afternoon in August when only parts of the M6 motorway were completed.

John had to do all the driving as this was a hired car and it was less than a year since I'd passed my driving test so I was not allowed to drive it. I'd passed first time; having taken a liking to the examiner and it being early closing day in town may have helped.

We stopped somewhere for a meal and then drove on to The Old England Hotel in Windermere. We were treating ourselves to a rather special place for our first night. And it didn't disappoint, the hotel or the first night.

It was wonderful to be together at last.

Our journey's end was Ullapool in the North-West Highlands of Scotland; narrow roads and a less than powerful engine made it seem a long way. It was.

At the end of our second day of travelling we were getting tired. Twilight fell, it was still some distance to our destination and the roads were narrow and winding. From time to time we had to slow down to walking pace as sheep on the road loomed up alarmingly in the car headlights.

We stopped for a second night at a bed and breakfast place at Spean Bridge where the corridors were punctuated with notices which told us NOT to take baths after such and such a time, to be PUNCTUAL for breakfast at such and such a time and NOT to make a noise.

When we crept down for breakfast the following morning, all eyes were upon us in the dining room. We felt ourselves to be the focus of attention as we were obviously on our honeymoon. No one said a word, they had read the notice which said, 'Do not make a noise.' Breakfast was eaten in a deathly silence.

We were glad to get away from there and start our final day of travelling. And what a day that was with the magnificent scenery of lochs and mountains spreading out before us. In the afternoon we finally arrived in Ullapool at the modest hotel we had chosen. Clean, bright and friendly. Perfect. We were there for about ten days, enjoying the scenery and walking on the mountains. And more than anything finally being together after our lengthy engagement.

One day we put a picnic in the car and drove out to the base of a mountain called Stac Pollaidh. Thinking we would soon climb it and be back by lunchtime we left the picnic in the car and started the ascent. It was much harder than we had realised and we didn't get back to the car until four o'clock. It's easy to underestimate distances in the mountains but on that day the Mars Bar I found in my pocket went some way to keeping our strength up.

Walking around Ullapool we bumped into some people, the Moffats, I knew slightly from Carrs Lane, the church I'd been going to in Birmingham. It turned out that they had a holiday cottage up there to which they invited us one afternoon. They were quite surprised when they discovered we were on our honeymoon.

They enjoyed walking as much as we did and a plan was devised whereby we would set off in two cars parking one at either end of a long walk along the coast near Achiltibuie. This involved leaving the Moffat family where we parked our hired car and then John driving Mr Moffat's very nice Wolseley saloon to the furthest point to which they would be walking, setting off ourselves to walk back to our car and returning their car keys to them when we met them somewhere along the coast. The scheme worked very well and meant that we all did the long stretch without having to go back on our tracks.

John was very visible on the hillsides on that holiday. We joked with the Moffats that they would have no difficulty spotting him among the heather when we were walking on the opposite side of Loch Broom to their cottage near Ullapool. Auntie Elizabeth and Uncle Ern had given John a bright orange shirt for his birthday.

The journey back to Nottingham was to be accomplished in two days with just one overnight stop. Money was getting short now and on the way south we looked for a cheap pub or guest house for the night. We couldn't find anywhere and ironically ended up in the most expensive hotel in Harrogate. Our little hired

Ford looked strangely out of place in the hotel car park among far superior models.

Since January we had regularly visited the building site where our new home was taking shape. We had hoped to be able to move into it as soon as we came back from our honeymoon but it was not to be. It wasn't finished in time but as John's mother was going to be away she said we could stay in her flat until the house was finished. So we went there after our journey from Harrogate. I was very nervous at seeing her now I was in my new role of daughter in law. But all went well; she slept in John's bed and we slept in her bed. A strange role reversal.

The next day we visited Auntie Grace in Brushfield Street where Auntie Elizabeth and Uncle Ern were staying until their imminent return to Canada. Uncle Ern had a late wedding present for us, a hammer. However, it was my birthday and when he found out he gave the hammer to me instead as a birthday present.

Elizabeth and her sister Lily, had married Canadian airmen soon after the First World War but they had crossed the Atlantic back to England on a regular basis apart from during the second world war. This time they were taking John's mother back with them for a three-month visit. She would be travelling out by ship and returning by air; very adventurous for her.

Within a few days the time came for their departure. John hired a larger car this time to accommodate his mother and the Canadian relations. Auntie Grace came too and we all went up to Liverpool. As we stood on the dockside waving the ship off poor Auntie Grace shed a tear or two. She would dearly have loved to be going too but someone had to stay behind and look after her brother Alf.

Three months later John hired a car again and with Auntie Grace we went to meet his mother at Heathrow. She'd had a wonderful time and had come back with a much more positive attitude to John's marriage. She turned out to be a very good mother-in-law and never interfered despite living only a mile or so away from us. I'm sorry to say that living so close to my mother would not have been such a happy arrangement.

Before we were married I had applied to Nottingham Education Authority for a position in a Junior School. The school I was allocated to was Berridge Road School which turned out to be the school that John's mother and Auntie Grace attended when they were children.

Auntie Grace still lived close by and sometimes at lunch time I would drop in to see her. Later we would visit her sometimes on Sunday afternoons and in the winter her house was freezing cold. We'd sit in the front room, rarely used, damp and cold. Two tiny lumps of coal smouldered on the fire and we all sat with our knees practically up the chimney trying to get warm.

As I have mentioned earlier Auntie's house had no

comforts of the modern age, no central heating, no hot water supply, no bathroom and a lavatory outside the back door down the yard. At least it was a flushing loo!

The school was a typical Victorian design with classrooms round a central hall. Until a few years previously a secondary school had occupied the upper floor but by the time I taught there the Junior school occupied both floors and the secondary school had a new building elsewhere. I had one of the downstairs classrooms and for morning assembly we went upstairs.

One morning when we came downstairs again I realised that my handbag had been interfered with. To my horror I discovered that £5, my entire weeks housekeeping money had been stolen from my purse. Of course, I should have kept my bag with me always and that taught me a lesson.

Berridge Road School and the surrounding area of Hyson Green was a big shock to me after my time at Green Meadow School. At that time, the area had the highest crime rate in the country. This was reflected in the behaviour of the children. Some of them were perfectly pleasant but some of the boys in my class had no idea of the difference between right and wrong and when I heard what they had been up to out of school I was shocked. Stealing from Woolworths among other places is one thing I remember and generally causing mayhem was another.

I was glad when the school bell went and I could make my escape. Mr Baugh, the headmaster, a strict disciplinarian, played golf every afternoon after school and used to give me a lift almost all the way home as his golf club was nearby. We finished school at 4pm and I'd see him waiting out there at five to four. No hanging around putting up displays or doing my marking then.

One day he told me that he'd spent some time in Canada and while he was there he had a dog that he was very fond of. When the time came to come back to England he had to leave the dog behind with friends. He looked in the rear-view mirror as he drove away for the final time and it nearly broke his heart to see his dog sitting in the middle of the road staring after him as if he knew he would not see his master again. Even strict headmasters can have soft centres.

Finally, our house was finished and we moved in. Building continued close by as houses and roads continued to encroach on the countryside. At first, we could walk around the corner on to the nearby fields where there were mature trees, hedgerows and banks with wild flowers growing on them but as the months and years went by it all became a sea of brick and tarmac. The attention to the landscaping of new estates that we have today was sadly lacking then. However, we were glad to have a house even though it was built on land that had recently been beautiful countryside.

Years later that whole area became totally built up and where once we had walked over the fields to John's mother's flat it all became yet another suburban area as Nottingham sprawled northwards.

At the end of October we had a house-warming party and as the street lights were not yet switched on I thought that the candles in the pumpkin heads I had carved out would look very jolly on the drive. That day the lights were finally switched on; well it was Hallowe'en so may be the ghosts and ghouls did need dispelling.

My parents came to stay with us for our first Christmas. The furniture John had made at Auntie Grace's house looked good as did the Broadwood piano that he had bought with money his mother had given him for his twenty-first birthday. During the Autumn we had one easy chair, oak-framed with a webbing base, which John had made but it didn't have any cushions. So we brought down pillows from upstairs to put on the chair and we took it in turns to sit on it. John was hurrying to finish another chair and the oak-framed settee. Meanwhile we had bought foam for cushions and I was making covers out of a brown tweedy material.

When my parents arrived on Christmas Eve Dad had to help John fix the webbing on the settee before it could be used. The floor had been bare boards since we had moved in but we had recently bought a blue Wilton carpet and were very proud of it. We couldn't afford a fitted carpet so the bare floor surround was stained dark brown.

For upstairs we had been given some old carpets. My parents assured us that they would be alright sleeping on camp beds in the spare room but the carpet in that room smelt of cats so I don't think their sleeping arrangements were very comfortable.

We did however have lovely curtains, Sanderson fabrics which had been made up at a very good curtain shop in Worcester.

Cooking for my first Christmas must have been rather fraught but I don't remember much about it. John's mother, Aunty Grace and Uncle Alf came for lunch and we proudly laid the teak table John had made with the fine china, glassware and cutlery that we had been given as wedding presents.

Uncle Alf ate in the kitchen so that no one would be embarrassed by his lack of table manners. I think he must have been a bit of a shock to my parents, as indeed he had been to me at first.

At that time my father had very firm opinions about handicapped people and people who were a social embarrassment. His views were that they should be shut away in homes, maybe mental hospitals, where they could languish and be forgotten. He certainly didn't want to see them and be reminded of their plight.

Years later when my mother had Alzheimer's he had changed his views, certainly as far as his own circumstances were concerned. He took her everywhere, especially onto the beach at Sidmouth where they lived and she was quite embarrassing at times. One's opinion on a given subject depends very much on where you are looking from.

In this case looking from the outside in at a

family's difficulty with a handicapped person one can feel very different as opposed to when you are in that position yourself and trying to cope to the best of your ability. There are times when brushing something under the carpet and pretending it doesn't exist, cannot sit side by side with a clear conscience.

On the Boxing Day of that first Christmas we all went to John's mother's flat for tea and when we looked out of the window before we went home we found it had started to snow. My parents went back to Birmingham the next day.

Early in the new year I discovered I was pregnant. That was a bit of a surprise. We had to do some urgent re-calculations of our finances as we still owed Dad the £200 he had lent us so we could have our honeymoon. We'd saved up part of the money and by being very careful we managed to send him a cheque in the spring.

One Saturday morning the post arrived early and we were still in bed. John went down to fetch it and there was an envelope with my father's writing on it. When I opened it lots of bits of paper fell out; it was the cheque for £200 torn up into many pieces. Dad had returned it to us and wiped off the loan. That was much appreciated and had it been an ordinary cheque that would have been the end of the matter but the problem was that it was a building society cheque and so to reclaim the money the pieces of paper had to be returned to him and he had to sign every single one. It was a very kind gesture; £200 in those days was a lot of money.

Another act of generosity from my parents was a washing machine that my mother bought for us during my pregnancy. Until then I was doing all the washing by hand in the kitchen sink. We didn't have a wringer and although we tried to squeeze as much water out of the sheets, towels and clothes as possible there was still a lot left in. During the winter when I couldn't dry washing outside it had to go on a wooden clothes rack we had bought and water dripped everywhere. The washing machine was a big help and when the washing came out after a good spin it no longer dripped.

Later, after the baby arrived, there was a lot more washing; disposable nappies were only just becoming available so it was the good old terry towelling nappies for our babies.

The baby was due on September 6th and I would be resigning from my job sometime in June. When I went to live in Nottingham I had to get a new dentist so I went to Mr James who had been John's dentist for years. His surgery was on Gregory Boulevard, just around the corner from Berridge Road School. Dental treatment was free during pregnancy and so before I left the school many of my lunchtimes during the spring term were spent in the dentist's chair having what seemed at the time to be a total refit of my many fillings. My mouth, full of instruments and rolls of cotton wool, I'd look at my watch and think I've got to be back in the classroom in fifteen minutes. Will I make it? I always did but it wasn't a very pleasant time.

There was no thought in those days of extended

maternity leave and then going back to one's job. You left work sometime before the birth, were paid a maternity allowance for so many weeks and that was it. Then for most woman you were a stay-at-home mum and looked after your baby.

When the time came to leave the school, at which I had been for less than a year, I wasn't sorry to get away from it. The staff had been friendly but the children and the surroundings were not very pleasant.

However, we hadn't planned to have a baby that early in our marriage, in fact I don't think we ever specifically discussed when we would start a family but as things turned out it was all for the best and I'm glad we had our children when we were young.

I felt at a bit of a loose end when I stopped work. What ever would I do each day? Soon after we were moved into our new home we acquired a kitten. We'd been admiring the two kittens our neighbours had and when they told us that there was one of the litter left and it was a male we decided that we would have it. Thus Charles came into our home. However, Charles turned out to be female and before many months had passed had her own litter of kittens in the airing cupboard on the landing. She had seven kittens and they kept us busy and amused for several weeks. When I was heavily pregnant they'd sit on my bump which could accommodate three or four of them. They used to climb all over the cushions on the settee and when they were all on the top it overbalanced and they all tumbled down. Fortunately we found homes for all of them and then had Charles neutered.

In July that summer I went to stay with my parents for a few days. I was pretty large by then and I think my mother was a bit embarrassed by my size. She'd never been pregnant herself and it must have seemed odd for her to be with her daughter who had been so thin when she was married only eleven months earlier. I was missing John and was glad to receive a letter from him telling me about the antics of the kittens.

After he finished school at the end of July we decorated the back bedroom which was going to be the nursery. John made a cot and it was painted white and had animal transfers stuck on each end. We put grey patterned linoleum on the floor, bought a baby bath, a pram and a carry cot and waited for the baby to arrive.

I didn't have far to go to the doctors for my check-ups as a new modern surgery had been built about five minutes' walk away around the corner. Dr McCracken was keen on home births and, as I wasn't keen to go into hospital, I was happy to settle for that.

For several weeks before the birth I went to relaxation classes where I was one of about twenty mums-to-be lying on the floor practising their breathing exercises. One by one the expectant mums disappeared and we'd hear that so and so had had a smashing baby boy or a gorgeous baby girl. We couldn't wait for our own deliveries as the hot days of August dragged on and we shuffled round like penguins with our distended stomachs.

One of the midwives giving the relaxation classes

was a small dark haired young woman wearing some robust scaffolding in the form of an impressive bra that pushed her boobs towards the sky as she strutted around on the highest stiletto heels I had ever seen.

When she came to inspect our brand-new nursery those same stilettoes dug tiny holes into our new linoleum and I was less than pleased. But what could I say or do? Within days I would be completely at her mercy when I was trying to remember what she'd taught us about how to breathe as I coped with my contractions.

On the morning of 30th August, I had backache and the odd strange feeling. Could I be having contractions?

While I attacked the huge pile of shirts that needed ironing, John got on his bike and pedalled round to his mother as fast as possible. At that time she hadn't had a phone installed.

She consulted her ever-handy medical book and they decided I probably was in labour. John jumped on his bike and cycled home even more quickly. He phoned the midwife in the afternoon when my contractions were more frequent and she came and gave me an injection of pethidine. While I dozed upstairs John spent a very boring evening looking at photos and drinking very strong tea with the midwife while not very much was happening upstairs in terms of the birth. Eventually she decided to go home but no sooner had she got into bed than things speeded up and she was called back.

Our son, David, was born at 6.30 am on Tuesday 31st August and was placed in the carry cot at the side of my bed.

It had been arranged that my mother would come and stay for a week or so to look after me and the household. She'd had her bag packed and ready to come for some time so they drove up as soon as John had phoned with the good news. He sent a telegram to his mother.

I was sitting up in bed feeling on top of the world, if a little sore in the nether regions, when my parents arrived. By the way my father crept into the bedroom I think he was expecting to see me lying in a darkened room with an ice pack on my head.

My mother's stay with us was a nightmare. She arrived, put on her overall and resumed her 'I'm in charge' mode. She meant well but she just couldn't adjust to the way we lived. Four years later my father felt she was beginning to lose it so I wonder if the dementia had already started then in a small way.

The way we lived was such a contrast to her life. She had help in her own home several days a week, the grocer phoned her every Monday morning for her weekly order which he delivered in the afternoon and there was no shortage of money.

The day came when I had to bath the baby on my own for the first time. I'd seen the midwife do it and now it was time to cope on my own. John would dearly have loved to be in on the first bathing of his son but I chose my mother instead. I thought she'd really love to be there.

I took my time over laying everything out that I would need but she was impatient for me to be getting on with it so it wasn't the fun experience it should have been. My stress levels were rising and there were tears that evening.

My mother said,

'There are often tears a few days after the birth due to hormonal changes.'

I knew about that but I think it was her attitude, not the birth that caused the tears.

A few days after David was born the Autumn term started and she had to cope on her own. John went back to school, cycling seven miles each way.

One day it was raining cats and dogs and he arrived home soaking wet and exhausted after a day at school and a dreadful ride home in the rain. She met him on the door step with the coal bucket.

'John, would you mind filling this up?' she said with a coy smile.

Yes, he did mind. Why couldn't she have just gone to the coal bunker herself and dealt with it, he grumbled to me.

An atmosphere was starting to develop and it wasn't helped the next day when we ran out of apples.

'There are no more apples,' she said. 'We'll have to get some more.'

'We can't get any more,' I said, 'I haven't any more money.'

'You'll have to ask John to give you some more,'

'He hasn't got any until pay day,' I replied.

She just didn't understand any more what it was like to have to go without because the money was gone.

When she finally went home we were barely on speaking terms and had decided that if we ever had any more children we wouldn't be asking her to come and help.

***

After we had moved in to our new home we decided to go to the Methodist Church in Bulwell. We were given a warm welcome by the congregation there and by the minister, Rev. Markham, so we decided to have David christened there. Family and friends gathered for the occasion which went well and the baby didn't cry very much.

The following spring when British Summer Time started the fact that church would be starting an hour early had escaped our attention and we arrived there just as the last hymn was being sung. How embarrassing that was.

One week-end that summer we noticed a crowd of people from the church going around the estate. It was hoped that before long people would be interested in a church being built on the estate. They were there to find out how much support for the scheme there would be. They discovered initially that about eight couples would be interested, not all of them being Methodists. But why wait for a church building people said? Why not meet in each other's houses?

So that is what we did and although at first people may have felt a bit embarrassed about praying, singing hymns and listening to a sermon in such close proximity to each other, eventually some close bonds were formed and when after three years or so the church was built and the house church services ceased I think we felt we had lost something.

A contribution we felt able to make to life on the estate was to start a youth club which was loosely church based. A couple called Gwen and David, who were part of the house church group, helped as well. There were still fields nearby and everyone went off to play rounders in the field and then came back to our house for refreshments afterwards and a short talk.

When our circumstances had changed David and Gwen took over the youth club. Later still when the church was opened in 1968 its minister Rev David Wheeler and his wife Elaine did valuable work on the estate. The church was an excellent building, designed, not just to be used on Sundays, but for the rest of the week too as a much-needed meeting place.

For David's first Christmas we went to Birmingham and had a tortuous journey to get there with the baby in his carry cot. Still counting the pennies, as we had to do for several years, we went on the X99 bus as we had done when we were engaged. It was a four-hour journey, door to door, tricky when you are breast feeding baby every four hours. The journey was made even worse by the fact that the bus broke down and all the passengers had to get off the bus and onto its replacement when it arrived. When we reached Birmingham, there was still the journey out to my parents' home on the service bus. The baby was constantly grizzling with hunger, milk was leaking from my boobs and I stuck a finger in his mouth to try to fool him that it was just what he wanted. It was a nightmare. I wished we had been able to afford a taxi.

My father's days of being stingy over the cost of phone calls seemed to have changed to generosity once we were married. Discussions had been under way about John going to university. Undoubtedly having a degree rather than just a teaching diploma, would advance his career. But there was no way we could survive financially on a student grant which even with allowances for a wife and child would still be at least £200 a year less than his teaching salary. However, it began to seem a possibility when Dad kindly offered to give John £200 a year for the three years he would be at University. John would have to supplement that by working in his vacations.

In the Autumn of 1966 John began a Geography degree course at Nottingham University. We bought a windowless black Ford van, it being the cheapest form of transport we could find and its dual purpose was to take John to the university and be a camping van for holidays. He fitted up the interior with benches and cupboards and we bought foam for cushions and covered them with a shiny red plastic material.

The first time we tried it out we went on a three-day holiday to somewhere near Dove Dale in

Derbyshire and forgot half the cushions. David was toddling by then and made friends with the cows on the other side of the fence. Fortunately we were only away for a couple of nights.

In the summer, carefully remembering all the cushions this time, we decided for our summer holiday to do a tour of our relations so that they could see the baby. Not much of the holiday was spent camping as we were able to stay with some of our relations.

We started in Birmingham where my parents enjoyed seeing their grandson and then moved on to see relatives in Devon, Bournemouth, Maidenhead and finally Ipswich where John's mother was staying with Auntie Win and her mother. John's Grandma was a delightful little old lady with a great sense of humour and she was very pleased to see her great grandchild. Finally, after our mammoth relation tour we went home. We took John's mother with us back to her flat.

During the Autumn I became pregnant again, with baby number two being due at the beginning of June. It was during that pregnancy that I became friendly with Julie who was expecting her first child a week or so before our baby was due. Julie was a speech therapist and had me in fits of laughter when she put on various accents especially a Brummie one. Later, after both our babies had been born, we went to keep fit classes together and shared a lot of laughter.

John's Part One exams were due to start on Monday 5th June. We could envisage him being called out of the exams because I had gone into labour. When

I went to see Dr McCracken on the preceding Friday I said to him,

'I hope this baby is born this week-end.'

When we were sitting in the garden that afternoon I felt my contractions start. Tim was born at 10.30 that evening giving John plenty of time to get David into bed and settled down.

True to what we had decided my mother was not asked to come to stay. John's mother came over every day and quietly got on with whatever needed to be done without making any fuss or interfering. She was an excellent mother-in-law.

Julie's baby, Kate, was born ten days before Tim and later we spent a lot of time together wheeling our babies to the park and playing with them in each other's homes.

Julie gathered together a group of like-minded young mothers and we started going to each other's home for coffee once a week. Almost all of us were young professionals who had given up our jobs to start a family. We enjoyed getting together and having some lively conversation. It was very easy for new mothers on that estate to feel isolated and when your conversation was mainly conversing with your toddler you might wonder if your brain was shrinking.

In the Autumn when Tim was a few months old we acquired our first dog. She was a black and white border collie and came from my cousin Mary whose dog had given birth to a litter of puppies. We called her Sheba, she lived to the exceptionally old age of seventeen and we were very fond of her. Those seventeen years saw a lot of changes in our lives with the children growing up and Sheba was with us all the time. We were devastated when she died.

After a few months I found a temporary teaching job nearby for one afternoon and one morning each week and Julie did a morning's speech therapy. We looked after each other's children while the other one was working and John's mother came to help too. As John was receiving a grant there was a limit on what I could earn before the excess was taken back. Just when I had reached that amount my job was axed. I felt pretty bad about it because I had enjoyed getting back, in a small way, into teaching. But financially, to have continued, would not have benefitted me at all.

When John's university term had finished we went to Abersoch in North Wales, just along the coast from Llanbedrog, the scene of many of my childhood holidays. Our holiday there cost us ten pounds; we were still counting the pennies. The weather was good and we found a nearby sandy beach. Tim was not yet walking so he played safely on the beach while we took three-year-old David into the sea. The toilets and washing facilities on the camp site were on the opposite side of the field from where we had parked the van and John took David over there with his yellow infant toilet seat. I was very amused one morning to see David wearing it like a crown on the return journey to the van.

David had been given a place at the local nursery

in the Autumn on the strength of me teaching nearby and fortunately, although I was no longer teaching, he was still able to keep the place. He started there in September 1968 going for mornings only. He was three and although he was a confident child, he looked very small when I left him there on his first morning. Other mothers were making a fuss but although I felt tearful I managed not to shed any tears, not in front of him anyway.

The black Ford van had by now been replaced by a blue Bedford van into which John fitted windows and rigged it up inside as a camping van.

John had to work in the vacations to boost our income. At Christmas he did the Christmas post, working in the sorting office or out on a round delivering Christmas cards.

In the summer he worked at a local concrete factory which was heavy, boring work. On another occasion he used his driving skills to deliver bread for Sunblest Bakery. The job entailed more than just bread deliveries for there were cakes to sell as well. His round took him out into the mining villages of Nottinghamshire. When he got back to the bakery often not all the cakes would have been sold and as the cream cakes could not be kept until the next day he'd stop in a lay-by somewhere and lick the cream out of them. He knew they would be thrown away anyway and he wasn't going to waste that cream.

In the Autumn of 1968, his final year at University he was due to go on a field trip to Italy. I became very upset as the time for his departure drew near. Of course I was going to miss him and wondered how I would get on coping with the children on my own but I think I also felt left out as he was going off to a wonderful location and I was missing out on the experience.

David Wheeler, our new minister and his wife Elaine, arrived to pick John up to take him to the station. They knew I was upset about him leaving and called in on their way back to make sure I was alright. They were a lovely couple.

John was twenty-five when he went to university and so was several years older than most of the students starting their degrees that year. There was a Nigerian student who, like John was older than the other students. His name was Robinson Ebisori who had left a wife and children behind in Nigeria. He wouldn't be seeing them for three years and what was particularly worrying for him was the civil war going on in Nigeria at the time. He didn't hear from them for a long time and didn't know whether they were alive or not.

He used to come and visit us from time to time as we wanted to make his lonely life away from his family a little more bearable. He couldn't understand our habit of leaving the baby crying in the pram and would get up and go and rock the pram. Maybe babies didn't cry in Nigeria, possibly they were tied to their mother's backs all the time.

I was very proud of my husband when he finally

obtained his degree in the summer of 1969. We had hoped that he would find a teaching position in Nottingham that would be a step up the ladder from the job he had had before. We didn't want to move away and leave his mother behind nor could we afford to move. But there was no suitable job and moving away seemed to be the only choice we had.

He applied to Education Authorities that would pay removal expenses and Kent replied by telegram. There was a job going at Fort Pitt Technical School in Chatham which would give John a step up the ladder. He went down for his interview and stayed at the Gordon Hotel in Rochester overnight. The interview was successful and while he was there he started to obtain information about housing in the area.

The first shock was that house prices in the south of England were significantly higher than they were in Nottingham but we knew we'd have to manage somehow. We didn't want to leave Nottingham; the overcrowded south-east of England was the last part of the country I wanted to move to.

We went down to Kent together to look at houses, leaving John's mother to look after the children with Julie agreeing to pop in at bath time and help.

We found a reasonable semi-detached house in an area called Lordswood to the south of Chatham. All seemed to be going well with the move until several weeks on the sellers of the house we had chosen pulled out and we had to go down to Kent again to find somewhere else to live. This time we decided it would be too much for John's mother to look after the children again so we took them with us and camped in our blue van near Headcorn.

In the end this worked out well as the house we finally bought near Chestnut Avenue at Walderslade was much nicer than the first house we had chosen. It had a public open space at the back and woods nearby.

In September we moved, rather unwillingly, to Kent but we assured ourselves that it would only be for a year or two and then we'd go back up north again. In the event we lived in Kent for the next thirty-eight years.

'Surely you have grown up now?' I hear you ask.

'Yes, of course I have, I'm twenty-seven but having got so far, I might as well go on almost until the time when I became a goat keeper.

Chapter Twelve
Life in Kent

So there we were in Kent in a semi-detached house at Walderslade. John had his new job to get used to and I knew nobody and felt lonely. Financially buying a house in the south had been a bit of a shock because the prices there were so much higher than in the north so our own finances were still tight.

One day in that first Autumn I saw an advertisement for a job at a Field Studies Centre at St Mary's Bay on the Kent Coast at Romney Marsh, a job that would help our finances considerably. John's application was successful and for several years he went off there for six weekends in the Autumn and three in the Spring. It involved taking groups of secondary school children and their teachers, mainly from London schools, around Romney Marsh to do Field Work.

The centre consisted of several large concrete huts, which were used for dormitories, the canteen and classrooms. John was allowed to take the family and it provided a short free holiday for us. We didn't go every week-end as it was sometimes very cold but while John was occupied with the school parties I would go off exploring in the blue van with our two boys, sometimes popping into the public loos at Greatstone where there was hot water at the basins, a bonus for frozen hands.

Interestingly it was at this centre at St Mary's Bay, between the wars, that the Duke of York, later King George the Sixth, was involved with camps for boys from mixed backgrounds, some from Public Schools and some from industrial towns.

David had his fourth birthday just before we left Nottingham where he had been attending nursery for a year and so I explored the possibilities of finding another nursery near to our new home. There was a nursery at Lordswood for teacher's children but as I wasn't teaching that was no good.

However not far away I discovered there was a pre-school playgroup that had sessions three times a week and I managed to get him a place there. A lady called Val Crawley was running it and the mothers of the children attending it helped her on a rota basis. Val lived just around the corner from where our house was so we often walked to the playgroup together. She had a son also called David; they were both very bright boys.

To build up my social life I took Sheba to a dog training class where she was promoted into the advanced class after only three lessons.

A man called John Stokes called on us. In his spare time he worked for the Kleeneze company, selling brushes and household cleaning products, as a source of extra income. He was a friendly man who knew a lot about the area so we told him we were looking for a church that had a creche. He attended St Luke's

Methodist Church in Rochester and he said they had a creche and a Sunday school.

We started going there and were welcomed by a group of very open -hearted people who were active in the community. John and his wife Violet were particularly friendly and from time to time invited us to dinner parties at their house.

David and Tim enjoyed going to the playgroup and the two Davids became good friends. Val, a trained teacher like me, was the ideal person to talk to about a choice of primary school for David who would be starting school the following September. She recommended St Thomas More's Roman Catholic School which is where her son David would be going. I subsequently found out that they accepted a certain percentage of non-Catholic children and were happy to enrol him there to start the following September, when he was just five.

A few weeks before the end of term Val told me she was going back to teaching when her youngest child, David, was at school and she asked me if I would like to take over the running of the playgroup. This was an unpaid job but I was happy to do it.

Val started teaching at St Thomas More's and after David started there in September I went into the school once or twice a week on a voluntary basis to help wash paint pots and do similar mundane tasks. Within a few months of moving to Kent and knowing nobody my life had become quite busy and I had met a lot of people.

A term or so later Val found she was expecting another baby and Sister Callista, the nun who was headmistress of the school, asked me if I would like to teach there as Val would be leaving in due course.

I hadn't intended to go back to teaching until the children were a bit older but it was too good a job offer to turn down.

The boys were growing up and enjoyed the large grassy area at the back of our house where they could race about and ride their bicycles. The blue van that John had put side windows in took us on holiday to St David's in Pembrokeshire in the summer of 1970.

My parents had moved to Devon around the time we moved to Kent and were now living in Sidmouth. My father had retired and they had bought a bungalow on a hillside above Sidmouth where there was just a glimpse of the sea from the dining-room window.

My mother had convinced herself that we would go there each summer for a fortnight by the sea. She was to be disappointed, partly because the beach at Sidmouth was mainly stony and crowded with holiday makers and partly because I didn't want to spend a fortnight with my parents. However we did go to stay with them for a few days twice a year.

In the summer of 1970 we went there first and then travelled on to St David's for a fortnight. We had never been to South Wales before so it was purely by chance that we had chosen William Lewis's farm at Rhosson not far from the Lifeboat Station at St David's. We arrived in a coastal mist which obscured the surroundings. All we could see was the camp site field and a few nearby hedgerows. When the mist had lifted the following morning we could see the hills, the sea and a very inviting track which we discovered led down to a beach called Porthsele which had golden sand and rock pools. It was perfect for two small boys, our dog Sheba and for us. They spent their time digging, exploring rock pools and clambering on the rocks.

That area was so ideal for holidays that we went back there for fourteen years, camping, caravanning and staying in cottages over that period of time. The boys became so attached to the area that they even went back there with their children in later years.

A pattern developed of going to Nottingham to see John's mother and down to Sidmouth in the summer holiday and to either Nottingham or Sidmouth in the Easter and Christmas holidays. We also received parental visits. John's mother came for a fortnight twice a year; my parents came for a shorter time.

It was on one of John's mother's visits in August 1970 when David had his fifth birthday that we went to Navy Day at Chatham Dockyard. At that time it was still a working dockyard and it was interesting to wander round seeing the war ships. John's mother very adventurously agreed to go on a tour of a submarine. When she got stuck on one of the narrow ladders a kindly sailor said to her,

'You've got to go up or down Madam. You can't

stay there when we go to sea.' I think she chose to go down and our tour continued and we were horrified to see the cramped conditions that the sub-mariners lived in.

The Dockyard was closed in 1984. The cobbled streets, the church and over a hundred Georgian and Victorian houses have made it a popular location for filming. Parts of Les Misérables, Call the Midwife and Mr Selfridge have been filmed there.

Chatham Historic Dockyard is now a maritime museum on part of the site. The working life of the dockyard in 1758 has been recreated, several ships can be toured, also The Ropery, a listed building which was the Georgian and Victorian rope factory. I once had a colleague whose father had worked there prior to the closure of the dockyard. It is a fascinating place to visit and transports the visitor through much of Britain's maritime history.

That Autumn I was pleased to be going back into teaching; apart from anything else the extra money would be very useful. However, there was a problem and that was finding a nursery for Tim who was only two and a half at the time. I have mentioned the nursery for teachers' children at Lordswood and that is where he went. Getting him there, which was in the opposite direction to the school I was teaching at, was quite a problem.

By this time John had taught at Fort Pitt for two years and had moved on to teach at Borden Grammar School in Sittingbourne where he was Head of

Geography. He took us to a point near to the nursery on his way to Sittingbourne. The teachers who ran the nursery came out from Chatham on the bus. As the bus went up the road to turn around I took Tim into the nursery where he stayed for the day and then ran with David to catch the bus as it came back down the road again. I had a few minutes to catch my breath before the bus dropped us near the school and we went in, just in time to start the day's work. Fine timing!

Eventually some mothers who lived near the nursery collected Tim for me and brought him down to the school at the end of the school day when they came to pick up their children from school. That was very helpful.

I used to read a story to my class at the end of the afternoon and a few minutes before school ended I'd hear the door open and a chubby smiling face would appear around the corner. Tim had arrived. He'd come in and sit on my lap during the last few minutes of the lesson and listen to the story. Afterwards the three of us walked home together. Later, Sister Callista allowed Tim to start school early so then the day started with a pleasant walk to school instead of the mad rush we'd had for a year.

I enjoyed my time teaching at that school tremendously. It was a bright, modern, single story building and the staff were all younger than me, apart from Sister Callista. Sister Callista was friendly as well as being a stickler for discipline but she was surprisingly broad minded. I was the only non-Catholic teacher on the staff. One day we were discussing hymn books in the staff room, maybe I had taken in a couple of mine, obviously not Catholic ones. Sister Callista said,

'They are not Catholic or Methodist or whatever, they are Christian hymn books.'

Good for her I thought. I was even allowed to teach Religious Education, not doctrine of course, but Bible Stories.

The time came when David and his friend David Crawley were in my class for a year. They were both very bright boys and keen to answer questions and participate in classroom life.

My son David would persistently put his hand up and call,

'Miss, Miss,' when he wanted to answer a question. In the end I said to him,

'David, am I running this class, or are you?'

He went on to be a teacher himself so did get to run his own classes eventually.

St Thomas More's was an excellent school with a high rate of achievement and very good behaviour. Every Wednesday all the pupils went to Mass at the church next door to the school. I found it very interesting and even as a non-conformist I found the basic communion service was very similar to that in the Church of England and many of the non-conformist churches.

What a shame in our churches we have placed so much importance on our differences and not what we have in common. Now, forty years later, when we are an even more multi-cultural society we need to concentrate on what the different groups in our society have in common whilst still celebrating and sharing our cultural differences.

I think the press is responsible for some of the discontent in society today. People's anger and violent demonstrations provide much more dramatic news than the good and peaceful events that are happening continually but don't reach the newspapers and television reports.

Having used the word violent I am reminded of one upsetting incident that occurred while I was at the school. Often first thing in the morning I would get the children to write their diaries, probably while I collected the dinner money. One Monday morning a little boy in my class who was aged about eight, came to me and said,

'Miss, I can't write my diary today because something happened at home at the week end that I am not allowed to talk about.'

I said,

'You can tell me because I am a teacher.'

He then showed me the back of his legs. I was shocked; his legs had been beaten until they were raw. This was in the days when little boys still wore short trousers and it was easy, not only to give them a quick smack if necessary, but to see if any corporal punishment had been overdone. Sometimes of course it happened where it could not be seen and that includes mental abuse, the results of which may be hidden for years.

The Deputy Head's class room was next door and in his class, he also had this boy's brother. When I went to tell him what I had seen he called the brother up and found that he had been beaten just as badly.

I often wondered if the NSPC should have been informed but Sister Callista said the priest would deal with it. At the time I wasn't at all sure that this was the right approach but with hindsight I think it was, as the priest knew the family and had an ongoing relationship with them. However today the police would have to be told.

When I started teaching again our financial situation improved and we were able to buy a spacious frame tent. The blue van was sold and we bought a Ford escort estate car; John made a trailer to carry the tent and our luggage.

The boys were growing and occupying more space. It was good to have this roomy tent, with its two bedrooms and a living area, to take on holiday. We continued to go to St David's but the weather wasn't always kind to us.

I used to make two Christmas cakes at that time, one being saved to take on holiday in the summer. After the children had gone to bed we used to sit with our piece of cake watching the tent groundsheet billow up and down.

The tent had large detachable doors with plastic windows at the front. We were sitting inside looking through the doors at the rain sheeting down outside one day when two boys who had been fishing, trudged up the field going from tent to tent to see if anyone wanted to buy the mackerel they had caught. I fear they didn't make many sales.

Although I had been most reluctant to move to Kent we felt that now we were living there we should make the most of living within striking distance of the sea. We explored Romney Marsh, visited the lighthouse at Dungeness which we reached on the miniature steam train from Dymchurch and explored the coast from Sandwich round to Deal, Ramsgate, Margate and Whitstable.

From there on round the coast there are numerous creeks, the Isle of Sheppey and of course, the Thames estuary near Faversham and Sittingbourne where sailing is a popular pursuit.

One day, while standing peacefully on the beach at Seasalter gazing at a plethora of little white sails bobbing on the sea, John dropped a bomb shell,

'How about us having a boat of our own?'

The boys, immediately alert and fresh from recently imagining themselves as sword-wielding Roman soldiers on a visit to Hadrian's wall in Northumberland, instantly switched to visions of themselves as swashbuckling pirates.

'Oh Dad, can we?' they chorused.

He looked at me and I realised the die was cast. There was no going back.

'Yes, it would be a great adventure,' I agreed,

making a mental note of the impending need for life jackets.

The male members of the family had enthusiastically taken up John's suggestion that we should have a boat of our own and we bought an Enterprise sailing dinghy which they enjoyed. I tried to show some enthusiasm but life on the ocean wave has never had much appeal for me neither does it today when the state of the sea has to be almost flat before I will agree to go to France by ferry.

John is always keen to have a project and after some time, when he and the boys had enjoyed the Enterprise, it was felt that I might enjoy sailing more if we had a small cabin cruiser. He borrowed a boat trailer and we went down to Dorset to collect the hull, mast and sails of our new boat which he then set about completing in the garage of our house in Walderslade. He started the project in the Autumn and worked on fitting it up with a cabin and whatever else boats need, during the winter.

That Christmas was memorable as our plans for going to Nottingham to spend the festive season with John's mother were put on hold when the boys went down with a dreadful sickness bug.

As we had expected to be away we had no Christmas food in the house and ended up having beans on toast for our Christmas Dinner. I think John even managed a session of boat building while the boys were recovering and then, finally we went north.

By the spring the boat was finished and a trailer

arrived to transport it to Conyer where it was launched and then moored. There then followed, in the words of Ratty in The Wind in the Willows, a period of 'messing about in boats', a pursuit that Ratty was extolling to his humble friend Mole. It was a pursuit that was new to us, the readying of the boat for the voyage, listening to the sound of the wind in the rigging, the gentle chug, chug of the motor as we went down the creek, the lift of the waves as we met the incoming sea and then the peace of the marshes as the sails were raised and the breeze took us forward.

One afternoon we set off on our great expedition, to spend a night on the boat. Ready with life jackets, food, bedding and spare clothes we boarded the boat in great anticipation. It had been decided that we would sleep aboard at the mooring in the marina and set off at high tide early the following morning. In the grey early morning light we readied the boat for the departure. Around us other people were doing the same with their boats, all keen to be off when the tide was right and the endless mud had been covered to a sufficient depth.

It was a misty morning when a line of boats left the marina and motored down the creek. As other experienced sailors who knew where the safe channels were, made their way out to sea we stayed inshore. There was no wind to blow the mist away, we couldn't see where we were going so we curtailed our adventure and before long, while the tide was still high enough to avoid getting stranded on the mud, made our way back to the marina. The boys spent some time playing around in the small rubber dinghy that was tied to the stern of the boat and then we went home. Not a highly successful trip.

Nor was another time when there was a lot more wind and we went down the creek and out into the estuary only to be caught in a squall when the boat tipped over alarmingly and the boys and the dog were shut in the cabin for safety. But all was well.

After that John decided the boat would be more stable if the keel was remodelled. So on a sunny summer's day we went down the creek and grounded the boat on Horse Sands not far from Harty Ferry taking care not to harm the shellfish beds We spent several hours playing on the golden sand while John took his saw to the keel of the boat. That was my kind of sailing, not even afloat where even the slightest motion of the sea would start making me feel queasy. Well I'd given it a go but it wasn't completely satisfactory. I was happier on dry land. Some years later another Enterprise was bought and towed to St Davids where John and the boys enjoyed sailing it.

A year after he became head of Geography at the Grammar School John started to take a Geography Field Trip away every year. He went to France three times, taking groups to Dinard in Brittany and St Jean de Luz down on the Spanish border near Biarritz in the Basque country.

But for me the trip to Souillac in the Dordogne was the most memorable. It was a combined trip with boys from his school and some girls and staff from Fort Pitt Technical School, at which he had recently been teaching in Chatham. Alan, a member of staff from John's school and his wife Diane were also on the trip and I went along with our children.

We went by coach to Dover then by ferry to France and by train to Paris. We caught the overnight train down to Souillac arriving quite early in the morning. We didn't see a lot of the girls as they went off with their teachers during the day and used a different part of the hotel.

There had recently been a smallpox scare and we all had to be vaccinated before we went. Diane and I held a surgery every morning to check on everybody's reaction to their vaccination. Interestingly John had chickenpox a few weeks before we went to France which apparently was the reason for the lack of reaction to his vaccination.

Souillac is situated close to the River Dordogne and at that time the main road through the town was a major north/south route with lorries and other traffic making the town very busy. The A20 Autoroute has been built since then and when we went back about three years ago the town was very quiet and the eateries that had been so busy on that earlier visit had lost much of their business. At least one supermarket had been built on the edge of town which had also contributed to the loss of vibrancy in the town centre.

On that earlier school visit we went by coach to Rocamadour, a fascinating cliff top village accessed from the parking place at the bottom of the cliff by the Grand Escalier, a staircase constructed from polished limestone in which we could see fossils. Rocamadour has been an important pilgrim destination for a thousand years. The shrine to the Black Madonna became famous for its healing powers and became a stop on the pilgrim route to Santiago de Compostela. Naturally gift shops abounded and Tim bought a tiny model of a tortoise made from half a walnut shell.

Sometimes John set field work for the boys to do in small groups and we were able to go off on our own. In the evenings he'd meet with the boys and assess the work they had done during the day and prepare for the following days' work.

We were lucky with the weather and had a succession of sunny spring days when we walked in the countryside. On one of them the whole group walked to Lacave along quiet country lanes where brown goats scampered in the fields, grass verges were a profusion of wild flowers and trees in spring green shaded the route.

We stopped for a picnic on the banks of the Dordogne near to the hamlet of Pinsac. The hotel we were staying at provided us all with individual picnics in little carrier bags. John, in his role as leader of the party, 'chef de group', had a special picnic with a small bottle of wine. Afterwards the cork was consigned to the river and we watched it start on its journey towards Bergerac and eventually, the sea.

I didn't go on either of the other school trips to

France but some years later en route to Spain we visited the pretty fishing port of St Jean de Luz where a boat hangs from the roof of the church of St Jean-Baptiste. Our hotel on the slopes above the town gave us a good view of the beaches and the sea. It's a charming place.

52. John, Susie, David, Tim and Sheba in 1968

53. Susie, David, Tim and Sheba at Abersoch 1968

54. The family at Walderslade, Kent 1970

55. Camping at St David's 1970

56. The boat John built

57. David, Tim and Susie in the cabin on the boat

58. Susie afloat

59. David and Tim at Conyer Marina

60. Susie and Inge at Canterbury Road Junior School,
Sittingbourne

Chapter Thirteen
On the Move Again.

During the time we lived at Walderslade there were nationally on-going discussions about the viability of building a third London airport in the Thames estuary at Foulness. Had the plans for this gone ahead the flight path would have been right over Sittingbourne where John was now teaching at Borden Grammar School.

In 1974 it was finally decided that an airport would not be built there and so we decided to go and live in Sittingbourne. This would save John a lengthy journey each day. It necessitated me finding a new job and the boys changing schools but this was well before they had started secondary school so it seemed feasible.

The house we chose was so close to John's school that he took Sixth Form discussion groups there and once, when Tim was ill in bed, he was able to nip home at morning break to check up on him.

St Stephens had been built in Albany Road in 1927. Set among Victorian properties, it had been built for Sittingbourne's first probation officer and was a solid-looking brick double-fronted house. It had two reception rooms at the front and a good-sized kitchen, off which was a coal store and a toilet accessible from the garden. There also a study with a small dilapidated conservatory leading from it.

From the central hall, an impressive staircase went up with a turn half way up and on the first floor there was a large bedroom at the front that faced down Central Avenue, and two other bedrooms. There was a bathroom with a large, old gas geyser for heating water and a separate toilet.

The house had no garage but at one side there was a driveway that led to a small car park used by offices in the house at the back and from that there was access to hard standing where we kept our caravan. By this time we had moved on from camping to caravanning.

On the other side of the house was a terraced area where eventually we built a garage attached to the house. At the back of the house was a good-sized garden, quite amazing really, as we were so close to the town centre. The soil was excellent and when we had cleared all the junk from the garden we grew vegetables and had a lawn and flower beds. We also kept a few chickens at the end of the garden.

That was the first of the three properties we have bought that has been in an appalling state when we have bought it. John was now realising that we could stretch ourselves financially by buying a decent sized house that had potential and that he could put a lot of work into and we would end up with a very nice home. On the two occasions that we have sold these properties they have turned out to be sound investments. The other one is our cottage in France in which we are still living.

We moved into the house in Sittingbourne just

after Christmas 1974, going down to Devon for Christmas to stay with my parents and then coming back and moving in almost straight away. Completion had occurred a week or so before the end of the Autumn term and John had been very busy working with a couple of friends to rewire the house. That was in the days before it had to be done by a qualified electrician but all the men involved were experienced at doing electrical work.

The house had been lived in by a single lady and her mother and had been rather neglected for years. It also smelt of cats. The staircase and a large window above it should have been quite impressive but when at some time it had been re-painted no-one had bothered to wipe the dog hairs off the surface first. So we were faced with a revolting mixture of thick black paint liberally mixed with dog hairs. The walls were an unpleasant shade of green.

They'd had new carpets from time to time which had just been nailed on top of the previous layers of carpet which had also been nailed down over the years. When we went over at the weekends before Christmas to try to make the place habitable I had spent my time prising nails out of floor boards and when I had finished that it took four buckets of bleach and water to scrub the floor of each room clean. There was a park up the road and the boys, both during those days and later, often used to go to play there.

As soon as the previous occupants had moved out John went in and dismantled the old geyser and removed the antiquated, stained bath and all the other fittings from the bathroom. I'm not sure that the occupants had entirely moved out at this stage. They should have gone by a certain time on that day but they hadn't and John had to get in and get going. Time was limited if all that needed to be achieved was achieved by the day our removal men were booked. So there was probably some shock when they saw the bathroom they had only just finished using being carried out of the front door.

Eventually the house had a proper hot water system and a very pretty bathroom with a hot water tank and airing cupboard in one corner, a new suite and a fluffy pink carpet. We were very proud of it. Unfortunately when my parents made a visit later that year my mother was well on the downward slide to Alzheimer's and left the basin tap running overnight. By the time it had been discovered by the boys first thing next morning the whole place was awash and water was running through the floor and into John's study underneath. Even the drawers in his desk were full of water and the important notes in them were turning into papier mâché.

He rescued as much as he could and spread sheets of paper out to dry on our bed while we were at work during the day. John was not pleased and my father was deeply embarrassed.

That was the only time he came to that house with my mother. Taking her anywhere was becoming very difficult. He continued to drive up from Devon twice a year but without her, for she had gone into the local cottage hospital to give him some respite

The garden of our new home had also been neglected with hedges overgrown and fences and walls riddled with ivy. A large wooden shed stood rotting to one side of the lawn and although it looked as if it would collapse at any minute it took ages to demolish and practically stood up on one corner at the end. Work continued on that house and garden for nearly three years and during that time we both had full time jobs.

Before we moved I had applied for a job at Canterbury Road Junior School in Sittingbourne. There were two applicants and the other one was a young woman, recently married. I heard later that I was given the job because it was thought unlikely that I would have any more children and therefore wouldn't be having time off for maternity leave or indeed would be leaving after only being there for a short time. I was there for eight years.

The school was a mile from our home in Albany Road and I walked there each day. It was, like Berridge Road School in Nottingham, built in the Victorian era and was of almost the same design with classrooms around the hall which was used for Assembly and PE lessons.

Off the hall at one end was the staff room and a toilet for the female staff. Teaching there was such a contrast to St Thomas More's where at twenty-eight, I had been the oldest member of staff apart from Sister

Callista. Here at Canterbury Road School I was the youngest member of staff and everyone called each other by their surnames, so it was Mr Simpson, Mrs Reynolds, Mr May and so on.

Mr May was the brother of our solicitor in Sittingbourne; he had a very weak chest. The poor man spent a lot of time coughing. He lived near Faversham with his brother and sister. Along the road from his house lived a Russian princess.

A new headmaster started the same term as I did. He came from the Midlands, was a similar age to me and had just got married. The older staff who were very set in their ways found some of his innovations difficult to cope with.

Before long a younger man was appointed as Deputy Head and he shook the old dears up even more by calling everyone by their first names. He also revolutionised the way classroom displays were organised, very much for the better it seemed to me. But this was the 1970s which I felt was a low time in primary school teaching. Calculators were in and the learning of tables and spelling was out.

'No need for that,' we were told, 'the children can look it all up.'

In my opinion that attitude to those basics led to the appalling spelling of a whole generation of people twenty years later.

The Project Based form of teaching was very popular. We borrowed big boxes of library books from the main library in Maidstone and if, for example you were doing a project on water, there would be forty to fifty books on anything from reservoirs to the availability of drinking water in Africa, to river patterns, to household plumbing systems to...well you name it, anything even loosely related to water.

Set up on display shelves at the back of the classroom the books and the children's' work could make a very impressive display. At that time the children were encouraged to look things up for themselves but a lot of guidance was needed in terms of question sheets in each book to put them on the right lines. So this was individual work rather than teaching the class as a whole. The project would start off with an introduction by the teacher to the project and what we were aiming for and then after a few weeks of individual research, work would be displayed, the children, hopefully would all have folders full of their written work and illustrations and there would be a decent display on the classroom walls and shelves. This was very interesting but required a much larger input from the teacher than standing in front of the class giving them a lecture, setting them an essay to write and then marking their work.

Some children responded well to this type of approach and enjoyed finding out information on their own but others were not well motivated. The older more traditional teacher might have difficulty with the increased noise level in the class that this approach entailed because the children needed to move around the classroom gathering information and there was plenty of opportunity to chat to their friends on the way. I enjoyed it but it was hard work and the saying about teachers needing eyes in the back of their heads was very true in this situation.

Eventually that headteacher went on to pastures new and another head was appointed. He discovered that I had been given a small increase in my salary for music at my previous school and ensured that I was given that too at this school. My piano playing was not great but there was an excellent pianist at the school called Laurie Mitchell who was a year or two older than I was. I ran a couple of recorder groups and Laurie and I took hymn practices together. We also played a major role in putting on school concerts and musical plays. He played the piano and I conducted the children.

Inge was a teacher with whom I became particularly friendly with. After I had been for my interview the previous November her son Tim, a pupil at the Grammar School, went to John and told him his mother was a teacher at the school where I had just been interviewed. The following January when term started I was most relieved, among the serious faces of the older staff, to have someone who was very friendly right from the start. That was thirty-three years ago and we are still friends; she became a very important person in our lives.

Soon after I began to teach in Sittingbourne we started visiting each other's homes and I remember one such visit was when John was away on a Geography Field Trip to the Forest of Dean. Inge's son

Tim was studying A Level Geography and was also away on that trip.

We had intended to live in the house in Sittingbourne for about ten years. When we had been there for three years all the modernisations were finished and it was clean, fresh and comfortable. The garden was productive, we were both within easy reach of our jobs and the shops in Sittingbourne were only about ten minutes' walk away.

We had no intention of moving to an unkempt, dilapidated bungalow, eight miles away along a single-track lane in the country but that is what we did. We left our comfortable town house for a very different life.

In so doing we began twenty-nine very fulfilling years of country living. Our family grew up there on our smallholding at Larch Cottage on top of the North Downs in Kent.

John's mother came to live with us in a purpose-built annexe to our cottage. She was finally able to leave the flat she had wanted to leave so many years earlier and she lived close to us for the rest of her life.

We had various animals, I kept goats and eventually we made a wonderful garden that we opened for charity under the National Garden Scheme.

In 2007, we left that life behind and moved to the interesting old Roman town of Chichester in West Sussex but we missed living in the country and a few years later bought La Vesquerie, a cottage in the north of the Pays de La Loire in France. We renovated the cottage and made a pretty garden and are still enjoying our life there.

In writing about my early years I have found that it was rather like peeling an onion; layer after layer brought more and more memories to the fore; events I hadn't thought of for years floated into my mind again.

Peeling an onion can produce tears and indeed these memories did produce some emotional moments. But I think the most interesting thing was that, with hindsight, I could re-evaluate relationships.

I remembered that the relationship with my mother was fraught with difficulties. I had been basing that memory mainly on my troubled teenage years when my mother was unwell and I was flexing the muscles of independence. I felt regretful when friends spoke of the close relationship they'd had with their mothers. Why hadn't I been close to my mother? Why hadn't I shed tears of sorrow when she died.

But when I was writing about earlier times I was glad after all, to remember that there had been good times when we had been happy together.

And Finally
Who do I think I am?

One day early in March 2004 I had dialled a number far away in a town in the Midlands. I was excited but I was nervous too. Would it be answered? If it was, I knew I would at last be talking to my half-sister, Edna.

This was the culmination of a quest I had been following for several weeks or perhaps I should say for years.

I'd always known I was adopted as a baby, that my natural mother had been a widow and already had a daughter, that my father was a married man and I was an illegitimate baby.

When I was forty-seven I had obtained my original birth certificate. I had found out that my mother's name was Hetty Colley and her maiden name was Voyce.

But it was another seventeen years before I pursued my search. My adoptive parents had given me a very good home and although my adoptive mother had died in 1981 my father was still alive and I felt it would be an act of disloyalty to find my natural family. He died in 1998 but it was another six years before I started to look for my natural mother.

What kick-started the search then? It was the

recent availability of on-line searches. Prior to that time searches for births, marriages and deaths would have entailed a journey to the registration district and then a lengthy search through the available records.

I sat down at my office desk, switched on my computer and started searching. I had been told my mother was a similar age to my adoptive mother so I guessed that she had been born between 1902 and 1906 and I assumed she married in her twenties. Armed with her maiden name and her married name, I looked for her marriage. Eventually I discovered that she was married in 1926.

I sent for her marriage certificate and found that she, Hetty Voyce, was married on nineteenth of June 1926 when she was twenty-two.

Now I knew which year she was born in, so her birth certificate was the next thing to obtain. From that I found she was born on seventeenth of January 1904 so she was just a few months younger than my adoptive mother.

It was unlikely that she was still alive and eventually after a lengthy search I found the registration of her death. She had died in 1981, a few months before my adoptive mother.

The arrival of her death certificate was quite momentous because not only did I discover that her daughter, Edna, had been present at the death but there was her actual signature and her address. Now I knew my sister's name.

I looked on the electoral roll at the address at

which she had been living when Hetty died and was disappointed to see that she was no longer living there. However, my husband, who is very observant, saw her name at another address in the same road. That meant she was still alive. Now what would I do?

It was a real dilemma. She was already in her late seventies. If I contacted her and found she was impoverished I would certainly feel I should help her. Did I want to risk that complication in my life? Anyway, perhaps she didn't even know her mother had given birth to an illegitimate baby. And if she did know, would she want that 'baby' to contact her.

But I very much wanted to make that contact so eventually I wrote to her enclosing a copy of my birth certificate. What a shock that must have been for her. Suddenly one morning she found herself opening a letter from the half-sister that had been in her life, very briefly, nearly sixty-two years ago.

Meanwhile back in Kent I was waiting to see if she would reply. Amazingly a letter came by return of post; she did know about me and she wanted me to ring her as soon as possible.

So, on that cold March day, at last we were talking to each other. She seemed to be just as excited as I was and we arranged that very soon my husband and I would go up to the Midlands to meet her.

What a strange journey that was; all the time I was in a state of disbelief. Was I really going to meet my sister?

Any thoughts we might have had about her being

impoverished were soon dispelled and as we approached her house along a leafy road we saw splendid residences in their own grounds and Edna's house was one of them.

I need have had no thoughts of any awkwardness; her warm personality assured that we immediately developed a strong rapport.

There were so many questions and over tea and cake we chatted for a long time. Some of the facts I discovered have been mentioned earlier in this story. She was also able to tell me my father's name; with illegitimate babies only the mother's name is put on their birth certificates.

It was amazing to see photographs of my mother; I had often wondered what she looked like. Pictures of her in her later years do show a resemblance between us.

After further letters and phone calls I met Edna again later in the year on my birthday. She gave me a birthday card, 'To My Dear Sister'. Well that was a first. I'd never had a sister before on a birthday.

Sadly, that was the last time I met Edna because she died early in the following year. I was so very glad I had found her just in time.

She had given me photos and names of my grandparents and other relations and the information enabled me to trace my family tree.

Having found Edna and explored my family tree I felt unsettled for a while. Which family did I really belong to? Who did I think I was?

Finally, I decided that Mum and Dad who had brought me up and all the family members I have written about here were my real family despite me not sharing genes with them.

Who do I really think I am?

Well, of course, I'm the Birmingham Girl who has finally grown up.

You might also enjoy:

From Goats to a Garden
Based on Susie's diaries of the years living in
Kent

and

Our Small Stone Cottage in France
This book describes how in later years, Susie
and her husband buy and renovate a cottage
in France

Both books available as e-book
and paperback